CONSULTATION ACROSS CULTURAL CONTEXTS

Consultation Across Cultural Contexts addresses the challenges that school psychologists face when working in unfamiliar settings and diverse cultural contexts. First establishing the necessity of understanding and respecting these contexts, this book provides both theoretical background knowledge and a wealth of technical and practical information, animated by firsthand accounts. Divided into sections that touch upon topics such as difficult teachers and the role of poverty, race, and class, the selections include examples from diverse school ecologies, schools in various states of transition, resource-challenged schools, and more.

Antoinette Halsell Miranda is Professor of School Psychology at The Ohio State University.

Consultation and Intervention in School Psychology Series

Edited by Sylvia Rosenfield

CONSULTATION ACROSS CULTURAL CONTEXTS

Consultee-Centered Case Studies

Edited by Antoinette Halsell Miranda

Routledge
Taylor & Francis Group

NEW YORK AND LONDON

First published 2016
by Routledge
711 Third Avenue, New York, NY 10017

and by Routledge
2 Park Square, Milton Park, Abingdon, Oxon, OX14 4RN

Routledge is an imprint of the Taylor & Francis Group, an informa business

Library of Congress Cataloging-in-Publication Data
Names: Miranda, Antoinette Halsell, editor of compilation.
Title: Consultation across cultural contexts : consultee-centered case studies /
    edited by Antoinette Halsell Miranda.
Description: New York : Routledge, 2016. | Includes bibliographical
    references and index.
Identifiers: LCCN 2015019628| ISBN 9781138797550 (hardback) | ISBN
    9781138797581 (pbk.) | ISBN 9781315757049 (e-book)
Subjects: LCSH: Educational counseling. | Minority students—Counseling
    of. | School psychology. | School psychologists | Multiculturalism. |
    Communication in education.
Classification: LCC LB1027.5 .C6228 2016 | DDC 371.4—dc23
LC record available at http://lccn.loc.gov/2015019628

ISBN: 978-1-138-79755-0 (hbk)
ISBN: 978-1-138-79758-1 (pbk)
ISBN: 978-1-315-75704-9 (ebk)

Typeset in Bembo
by Apex CoVantage, LLC

CONTENTS

FOREWORD

Work in today's schools is increasingly exciting and challenging at the same time. Schools are called upon to ensure the educational success of vast numbers and types of learners who come from a wide range of cultural backgrounds, home languages, levels and qualities of previous educational experience, and diverse communities and ecosystems. Consultation is one way to professionally support the people who are educating our children. School consultation is a service whereby trained school professionals offer supportive services to the adults who are responsible for children and youths. Culturally competent consultants can assist in the development of interventions and approaches to improve the academic, behavioral, and social–emotional outcomes for children in schools.

The children in U.S. schools are far more culturally and linguistically diverse than the professionals teaching and serving them. In fact, the vast majority of teachers and school psychologists are classified as non-Hispanic White. Most (90.7%) school psychologists are White or Caucasian (Castillo, Curtis, Chappel, & Cunningham, 2011), and 82% of public school teachers are non-Hispanic White (National Center for Education Statistics [NCES], 2013), yet only half of the nation's school-age children are non-Hispanic White (NCES, 2013). In some states, such as California and New Mexico, only 29% of the students are from non-Hispanic White backgrounds (Aud, Fox, & KewalRamani, 2010).

Professionals and paraprofessionals in schools have their hands full in trying to meet the needs of the students in their schools and to better equip themselves with the knowledge and skills to achieve positive educational outcomes. Some schools have very limited financial and educational resources available to address student learning. Regardless of the diversity and levels of poverty of the students' families, there are huge disparities in the funding allocated to schools from one state to the next. For example, the annual dollars spent per pupil in Wyoming

($17,397) is more than double that spent in Idaho ($6,753), and schools within high-poverty communities tend to have less funding per pupil than schools in communities with moderate and higher levels of income (Baker, Sciarra, & Farrie, 2010).

Newell, Nastasi, Hatzichristou, Jones, Schanding, and Yetter (2010) described the gap between the professional standards, which include cultural competence in the standards for training and practice and the preparation provided by training programs, which have much less focus on multicultural competency development. Hazel, Laviolette, and Linemen (2010) studied the consultation course syllabi among participating American Psychological Association–approved school psychology programs and reported that 76–80% of the responding programs included less than 10% of course time for multicultural skills. There is a need to increase the multicultural competence of educators and for more global perspectives in the training and education of consultants (Ingraham, in press).

Since the 2000 *School Psychology Review* special issue on multicultural and cross-cultural consultation in schools, there has been more attention paid to the unique challenges and processes in providing consultation across cultures and within culturally diverse settings. Research has highlighted the need for consultants to receive training that specifically focuses on how to address cultural factors in consultation (e.g., Ingraham, 2003; Newell, Newell, & Looser, 2013). There is a need for more focus on the preparation of school consultants to attend more fully and competently to cultural factors in diverse school consultation practice. Training programs need to do more to teach consultants the knowledge and skills needed to work competently in today's multicultural schools.

This book offers valuable tools for the education of professionals to provide competent consultation in today's diverse schools, and it helps fill important needs in the profession. Dr. Antoinette Miranda and her students are addressing the issues of multicultural consultation in a diverse urban school context by using an ecological approach, grounded in the works of Bronfenbrenner (ecological model, 1989) and Bandura (reciprocal determinism, 1986) and the multicultural school consultation (MSC) framework (Ingraham, 2000). I believe that the combination of these approaches offers an important foundation for consultations in schools and that case studies offer rich material for developing consultants.

Through examination of the culture of the school and issues of communication, relationship, and diversity, in addition to the stages of consultation, different layers and dynamics are revealed. I have been using case studies in my own teaching and training of school consultants for a number of years. I find that the cases bring the various consultation techniques and approaches to life, making the learning of complex issues and themes more accessible. Through case presentations, learners are able to conceptualize the whole process of consultation from start to finish. Sometimes cases help readers conceptualize ways that an individual consultation can transition into systems-level interventions, an important consideration when issues of social justice, educational equity, and systems-level factors are impacting student success. Readers can explore the thinking and choices made by consultants, use these to expand their own understanding, and test out their thinking about consultation stages and processes. Like Dr. Miranda at The Ohio State University, I also use an ecosystems approach as a foundation to examine how contextual and systemic factors influence the members of the consultation constellation and also the settings in which their consultation occurs. At San Diego State University, my students do case analyses to apply the MSC framework to their own consultation cases in their school fieldwork and practicum placements. We analyze processes of consultation and communication across and within a variety of cultures. The MSC framework provides guidelines for working with numerous types of consultation constellations, where culture is distributed across the members of the consultation in a variety of ways. MSC attends to the reciprocal and transactional relationships among the consultant, consultee(s), and client(s). The cases in this book are useful in exploring some of these constellations, especially situations in which the consultant and consultee are from the same culture and are culturally different from the client.

MSC is a framework that is not tied to a specific model of consultation; thus, the concepts can be applied to multicultural and cross-cultural consultation through a variety of models, including consultee-centered, behavioral, and instructional consultation. The consultants in this book use a combination of consultee-centered and behavioral consultation in schools where the students often differ racially and culturally from the educators that teach them. For example, many of the cases involve schools in which the majority of the students are African American and the majority of the teachers are European American or White, thus providing examples of cross-cultural and cross-racial consultation in urban settings.

In meetings over the past decade of the Consultation Trainers Network and the Consultee-Centered Consultation Interest Group, consultation trainers and practitioners have asked for additional materials to help teach the knowledge and skills of effective consultation. This book, along with the recent books by Rosenfield (2012) and Sandoval (2014), gives readers concrete descriptions of consultation designed for today's diverse schools. Through the case presentations, readers can learn about some of the pivotal influences of poverty, race, language, cultural competence, and social justice as they are expressed in real consultation practice. I also think that the use of cases from developing consultants makes the process more approachable for others learning or expanding their proficiency to consult in schools. The more tools that are available to support consultation learners in their professional practice of school consultation, the better prepared consultants will be to serve the students, teachers, and families in schools and communities.

Colette L. Ingraham

References

Aud, S., Fox, M., & KewalRamani, A. (2010). *Status and trends in the education of racial and ethnic groups* (NCES 2010–015). Washington, DC: U.S. Department of Education, National Center for Education Statistics, U.S. Government Printing Office. Retrieved April 15, 2015, from http://nces.ed.gov/pubs2010/2010015.pdf

Baker, B. D., Sciarra, D. G., & Farrie, D. (2010). *Is school funding fair? A national report card* (3rd ed.). Newark, NJ: Education Law Center. Retrieved April 12, 2015, from www.schoolfundingfairness.org

Bandura, A. (1986). *Social foundations of thought and action: A social cognitive theory.* Englewood Cliffs, NJ: Prentice-Hall.

Bronfenbrenner, U. (1989). Ecological systems theory. *Annals of Child Development, 6,* 982–1022.

Castillo, J. M., Curtis, M. J., Chappel, A., & Cunningham, J. (2011, February). *School psychology 2010: Results of the national membership survey.* Presentation at the annual convention of the National Association of School Psychologists, San Francisco, CA. Retrieved April 15, 2015, from http://www.nasponline.org/advocacy/Mbr_Survey_Results_2011_Conv_Session.pdf

Hazel, C. E., Laviolette, G. T., & Linemen, J. M. (2010). Training professional psychologists in school-based consultation: What the syllabi suggest. *Training and Education in Professional Psychology, 4,* 235–243.

Ingraham, C. L. (2000). Consultation through a multicultural lens: Multicultural and cross-cultural consultation in schools. *School Psychology Review, 29,* 320–343.

Ingraham, C. L. (2003). Multicultural consultee-centered consultation: When novice consultants explore cultural hypotheses with experienced teacher consultees. *Journal of Educational and Psychological Consultation, 14,* 329–362.

Ingraham, C. L. (in press). Training and education of consultants: A global perspective. In C. Hatzichristou & S. Rosenfield (Eds.), *International handbook of consultation in educational settings.* New York, NY: Routledge/Taylor & Francis Group.

National Center for Education Statistics (NCES). (2013). Table 209.10. Retrieved April 15, 2015, from http://nces.ed.gov/programs/digest/d13/tables/dt13_209.10.asp

Newell, M. L., Nastasi, B. K., Hatzichristou, C., Jones, J. M., Schanding, G. T., & Yetter, G. (2010). Evidence on multicultural training in school psychology: Recommendations for future directions. *School Psychology Quarterly, 25,* 249–278. http://dx.doi.org/10.1037/a0021542

Newell, M., Newell, T. S., & Looser, J. A. (2013). Examining how novice consultants address cultural factors during consultation: Illustration of a computer-simulated case-study method. *Consulting Psychology Journal: Practice and Research, 65,* 74–86.

Rosenfield, S. (2012). *Becoming a school consultant: Lessons learned.* New York, NY: Routledge/Taylor & Francis Group.

Sandoval, J. H. (2014). *An introduction to consultee-centered consultation in the schools: A step-by-step guide to the process and skills.* New York, NY: Routledge/Taylor & Francis Group.

ACKNOWLEDGMENTS

I wish to personally thank the following people for their contributions to my inspiration in creating this book. First and foremost, I wish to thank Dr. Sylvia Rosenfield, who encouraged me to write the book. Without her encouragement, guidance, and support, I'm not sure it would have happened. Her belief that this type of book was necessary for the consultation field motivated me to develop a book that could be beneficial to the many students and practitioners who wish to engage in practice that addresses the many inequities that exist in our schools. I want to thank my training program, the University of Cincinnati, which introduced me to the multiple facets of consultation and its importance to indirect service delivery at a time when consultation was emerging in the field as an important and viable role for school psychologists. I want to thank the many students I have had the privilege to teach, guide, and mentor who have graduated from The Ohio State University school psychology program. They, without a doubt, kept me on my toes and always made me bring my "A" game to the table. A special gratitude goes out to the chapter authors who are the major contributors to this book. Their willingness to write about their authentic experiences as novice consultants, I hope, will inspire others to not only understand the importance of the multicultural school consultation (MSC) framework but also incorporate it into their everyday practice. A special thanks to Dr. Emilia Lopez and Dr. Colette Ingraham for their contributions to the book. I know how incredibly busy they are, but having the leaders in multicultural consultation as contributors is humbling. They have committed much of their careers to writing about the importance of MSC in the consultation literature, and for that I am grateful. A special acknowledgment goes to my colleague Dr. Kisha M. Radliff, who contributed to the social justice chapter. Like our many collaborations in the area of social justice, this chapter again allowed us to think about what it means to have a social justice mind-set.

And, finally, I would like to thank my family: my parents, A. C. Halsell and the late Charlotte Halsell, who gave me the gift of education and the belief that I could do anything in life, and my wonderful husband and children, Jim, Michelle, and Jimmy. They are a constant reminder that family is the most important asset we have in life.

INTRODUCTION

Consultation With Diversity in Mind

Antoinette Halsell Miranda

Consultation has been a desirable role for school psychologists for well over 40 years. Studies have consistently shown that this is a preferred role of school psychologists and one that can be effective in remediating academic and behavioral problems of students. There have been numerous articles written about consultation, from preferred models to the efficacy of consultation services in the schools, but there has been limited research on consultation in a cultural context.

In 2000, *School Psychology Review* published a miniseries devoted to cross-cultural consultation. It not only presented research in an area that had been limited to date but also employed practice-based inquiry that broadened our knowledge base in cross-cultural consultation (Rogers, 2000). Ingraham (2000) provided a conceptual framework for multicultural and cross-cultural consultation in schools that has guided much of the multicultural work in consultation. Other studies focused on the cultural embeddedness of consultation (Sheridan, 2000) and the importance of using qualitative methodologies such as naturalistic observation and case studies to better understand school-based issues in a cultural context and through a multicultural lens. Rogers (2000) suggested that scholarly inquiry in consultation is needed to meet two objectives: (a) examination of the practice of consultation in naturally occurring settings and (b) consideration of how cultural factors may potentially impact the delivery of consultation services.

Much of the early multicultural consultation literature often focused on the race or ethnicity of the consultant and consultee and its impact on the process of consultation (Gibbs, 1980; Pinto, 1981). More recently, in their work, Newell, Newell, and Looser (2013) have focused on how novice consultants address cultural factors in consultation. The results of their study suggested that novice consultants needed training on how to raise cultural topics with consultees and ask questions or collect data on cultural factors and the need for opportunity to practice these skills. Their studies were done with simulations, however, not in natural settings.

While there are many books in the field of school-based consultation, there are few that provide case studies for students. As Rosenfield (2012) suggests, most texts have focused on theoretical models of consultation and associated intervention procedures. She has written one of the few books that had a case study approach that supports the skill development of students in training. Case studies can be a powerful and effective training tool because they are stories that provide the reader with a realistic and contextually rich situation. They are an excellent way to bridge the gap between theory and practice.

Purpose of the Book

The premise of this book is to provide students in training as well as practitioners with case studies of real consultations that have occurred in culturally diverse settings. This book will take a broader view of how culture impacts consultation beyond the exploration of racial factors in consultant and consultee interactions. Ingraham (2003), in the *Journal of Educational and Psychological Consultation*, examined novice consultants' exploration of cultural hypotheses with experienced consultees through the use of case studies. She suggests that there is a need for qualitative methods to study the complexities of culture and that case studies are a good method of choice for such inquiry. Case studies can also capture the complex and multifaceted nature of culture that is often difficult to convey in an academic text. Most consultation books do not address the broader issue of diversity, and when they do address diversity, it is at an abstract level, meaning that there are few examples to illustrate how this might play out in real situations. Generally, the multicultural consultation framework (Ingraham, 2000) is illustrated but rarely with examples of how this is utilized in practice. This case study book will assist students in understanding how to apply the multicultural consultation framework, exemplify the challenges as well as lessons learned in terms of outcomes, and illustrate the complex nature of weaving through the multicultural maze to understand how issues of diversity may very well impact the implementation of interventions as well as the outcomes.

The cases presented were completed by students in a consultation course with a focus on behavioral interventions. One case was completed by an intern who still considers herself a novice consultant that examined consultation within a problem-solving team framework. As novice consultants, not only were they learning the *process* of consultation but also the *skills* used to examine the case through a multicultural lens using the multicultural consultation framework as their guide (Ingraham, 2000). This required the novice consultant to have the ability to identify, acknowledge, and work through the cultural context of consultation experiences. These cases go beyond the race or ethnicity of the consultant and consultee and examine the context of the diverse setting and its impact on the consultation process and the key stakeholders (consultant, consultee, and client). A consultant's ability to be proactive in identifying diversity issues and finding ways to overcome them is essential in maximizing the consultation process. The goal is to assist school psychologists and other school professionals in effectively engaging in consultation by understanding the multiple dimensions of diversity in school settings that may impact the process.

Consultation Framework

The school psychology program at The Ohio State University (OSU) has an urban and social justice focus. The OSU program is committed to preparing school psychologists to not only work in suburban and rural areas but to also acquire a better understanding of the psychological and educational dynamics related to stressors in urban settings. Recognizing that children in urban areas experience additional challenges related to population density (e.g., poverty and family and community violence), the urban specialty focus allows students to understand issues of poverty in particular and how these issues influence the lives of children in any setting. The specific framework used as the overarching philosophy to the program is the ecological model based on both the works of Bronfenbrenner (1989) (ecological model) and Bandura (1986) (reciprocal determinism), and it focuses on the multiple systems in which children exist. Thus, it would seem natural that the ecological consultation model be taught in the consultation class.

The ecological model examines the broad environmental contexts that influence both the academics and behaviors of a student. It recognizes the embedded systems that may potentially influence students' learning and behaviors in the educational system. The ecological model

> recognizes that utilizing the knowledge gleaned from examining the spheres of influence that have an impact on the child's functioning at school (microsystem, mesosystem, exosystem, and macrosystem) will likely result in a richer, more nuanced, and incisive identification of the problems that child may be experiencing.
>
> (*Erchul & Young, 2014, p. 491*)

This is particularly important in culturally diverse environments in which relationships are important, as well as understanding the impact and/or influence that issues of race or ethnicity, poverty, and culture, just to name a few, may have on learning and behavior. The problem-solving process is viewed as a critical structure in guiding the consultant through the development and implementation of an intervention. In moving through this process, emphasis is placed on examining the identified problem from an ecological perspective so that all identified factors that may be contributing to the problem are identified.

The multicultural school consultation (MSC) framework is used in concert with the ecological model of consultation. It is described by Ingraham (2000) "as a framework or lens for understanding the influence of culture on consultation [rather] than as a distinct model of its own" (p. 326). It is this framework that students are trained to use as a guide for understanding potential issues of diversity that may occur throughout the consultation process. The MSC framework consists of five components that are " designed to support a broad understanding of the theory and practice of multicultural school consultation" (Ingraham, 2000, p. 326). The five components are:

Component 1: Domains for consultant learning and development
Component 2: Domains for consultee learning and development
Component 3: Cultural variations in the consultation constellation
Component 4: Contextual and power influences
Component 5: Hypotheses about methods for supporting consultee and client success

Component 1 consists of eight domains that are necessary for consultant competence in multicultural consultation. The eight domains following Ingraham, 2000, are:

1. Understanding one's own culture
2. Understanding the impact of one's own culture on others
3. Respecting and valuing other cultures
4. Understanding individual differences within cultural groups and the multiple cultural identities prevalent in many individuals
5a. Cross-cultural communication
5b. Multicultural consultation approaches for developing and maintaining rapport throughout consultation
6. Understanding cultural saliency and how to build bridges across salient differences
7. Understanding the cultural context for consultation
8. Multicultural consultation and interventions appropriate for the consultee and client

This component would seem to be foundational to being able to utilize the other components of MSC. As such, it is important for the consultant to have training in the area of cultural diversity to be able to achieve the competency identified in Component 1. All of the novice consultants featured in this book took a diversity class the semester before the consultation class. A particular emphasis of the course was placed on students gaining self-awareness around issues of cultural diversity as well as expanding their knowledge base around a variety of cultural diversity topics, including poverty and oppression. Domains 1–5a were accomplished in the diversity class, whereas Domains 5b–8 were addressed throughout the consultation class. Throughout the case studies, novice consultants drew on this training as they attempted to understand the many diverse issues from an ecological perspective that potentially had an impact on their cases.

Component 2 is focused on the consultee and his or her needs as they relate to understanding the multicultural context in which they teach. There are four domains for consultee learning and development: knowledge, skill, objectivity, and confidence. These areas provide a broader lens for understanding when and how to intervene with a consultee who may need assistance in helping them intervene in appropriate ways that honors the cultural differences that might exist within the environment and with the client.

Component 3 considers the variations in the cultural composition of the consultation triad. These include consultant–consultee similarity, consultant–client similarity, consultee–client similarity, and three-way diversity: tricultural consultation. One of the key points that Ingraham (2000) makes is that it isn't the cultural identity of the individual that has an impact, but the cultural saliency (cultural similarities or difference perceived by consultation members) that determines which cultural variation matches a consultation constellation. The goal is always to build rapport and a positive relationship; however, stereotypes and lack of cultural understanding can make for a tense consultation relationship.

Component 4 addresses the cultural context in which schools and communities reside. It helps the consultant consider the impact of influences by the larger society, such as norms and values that may exert pressures on the consultation process in a variety of ways, both negative and positive. In addition, this component addresses issues of power and privilege that may exist between consultation members as a result of factors such as age, gender, race, language, etc., that may disrupt the balance of the relationship. The goal in the relationship is to have a coordinate status that promotes a true collaboration.

Component 5 is focused on hypothesized methods that promote the successful implementation of interventions through the support of both the consultee and client. Ingraham (2000) has identified several methods based on previous research that might assist the consultant in engaging in effective consultation in a cultural context. For example, one of the suggested methods is to seek cultural guides and teachers in the community who understand the cultural context of the school to provide feedback on your approach in consultation. Unlike the other components, this component is more focused on encouraging future empirical investigations to evaluate the effectiveness of these proposed strategies.

Consultation in Urban Schools

All cases were conducted in urban elementary schools. I had developed relationships with a number of elementary schools, most often through professional development. For several of the schools, the professional development has focused on training teachers in the problem-solving model. Thus, some teachers did understand the process of problem solving. Entry into the school is made through a request for teachers through the principal to participate in consultation to assist with a problem behavior in their classroom. It should be noted that teachers are also informed that the activity will potentially assist them in learning to develop effective interventions. In fact, this is the reason most teachers choose to take part in consultation in that they are hoping to find ways to intervene with students in their classroom. In addition, many teachers were seeking consultation because they expressed that they were not as well versed in behavioral interventions as they were with academic interventions.

Students are not only novice consultants to the consultation process but also novices to engaging in practices in which they are exploring the impact of diversity from multiple perspectives. While the course provides an understanding of the theories and processes involved in the consultation process, applying the principles to an actual case can be daunting for a novice consultant. Most often, students become focused on having an "intervention work" rather than the process of consultation in which they are engaged. From the outset, it is made clear to students that what is most important is for them to self-reflect on the consultation process and to apply not only the problem-solving model but also the MSC framework. They quickly realize that in the "real world," concerns and difficulties arise throughout all phases of the problem-solving process. In addition, there is an understanding that their status as "students" presents a myriad of concerns that challenge them as well (Newman, 2012). Supervision by both faculty and supervising doctoral students is critical in providing the necessary feedback to address the variety of concerns that are presented throughout the consultation process. Students are required to video their consultation sessions in which they provide a self-assessment; faculty and doctoral students also provide feedback. These have been invaluable for novice consultants to make improvements, particularly in the area of communication skills.

Case Studies

As students embark on their cases, they are guided through coursework and role plays that provide the essential structures and practices that are necessary in consultation. With respect to diversity, a foundation for understanding issues of diversity occurs in a course taken by students in the semester prior to the consultation course, which was referenced earlier in the chapter. The diversity course has a number of objectives that are beneficial and important for being able to apply the MSC framework. The course is designed for students to (a) develop an awareness and sensitivity to their own cultural heritages and to value and respect differences; (b) explore issues of racism, prejudice, oppression, and discrimination as they occur in the United States and understand the impact these have on culturally different individuals; and (c) understand how a child's cultural background can impact or influence his or her participation in the educational system. The consultation class further expands upon this foundation by examining research on students of color in education, particularly as it relates to behavior. As a result, students have a knowledge base that enables them to utilize the MSC framework as part of the consultation process. Even with this knowledge base, students are challenged to accurately identify those issues of diversity that might impact the case. The case studies will demonstrate how students navigate their way through issues of diversity; the challenges that they are faced with; and the lessons learned, including how they might approach a similar situation differently in the future.

The case studies detailed in the chapters begin by sharing the school's culture or ecology. This is especially important for urban schools, as many of them are experiencing rapid change and reform related to closing the achievement gap and exist in communities that have significant challenges. Additionally, novice consultants become knowledgeable of the demographics of the students, teachers, and the community. Some of this background, especially regarding the trajectory of the schools, is shared prior to their entering the consultation process. Students gather more information from the school's report card, consultation sessions with the consultee, observations in the classroom and school, interviews with the principal, and community mapping. Novice consultants are continually challenged to examine all of these variables in a cultural context as they work through their cases. Supervision becomes an important variable as they seek answers to questions they may have regarding potential cultural conflicts that might arise. While some of the cases are from the same school, students may present the schools slightly differently given their own lens and what information was collected that formed their perspective about the school's culture and ecology.

The chapter authors discuss the important elements of relationship building with their consultees, which is a critical element of school consultation (Erchul & Young, 2014). Communication skills are one of the most important aspects of building a positive relationship in which trust is built with the hope of promoting a cooperative partnership. Both verbal and nonverbal communication skills are emphasized, with particular emphasis on developing effective and skillful questioning, paraphrasing, and summarization that will assist them as they move through the problem-solving process. The authors share the challenges and successes they had in utilizing their communication skills.

The crux of the consultation process is the problem-solving model. One of the most challenging aspects of the model is problem identification. One needs to understand a variety of contextual factors (Zins & Erchul, 2002), which is even more complex when there are issues of diversity. Furthermore, as students attempt to analyze the problem from an ecological perspective, they are continually challenged to simultaneously incorporate the MSC framework to determine if issues of diversity have an impact. In many ways, the ecological perspective complements the MSC framework, and I believe that these naturally fit together. This really provides students guidance in terms of how to think about diversity in broad ways from multiple perspectives, especially beyond consultant–consultee race issues. Particularly, as the authors are novice consultants, the case studies demonstrated the successes as well as missteps along the way in attempting to identify accurately diversity issues, whether direct or indirect, that had an impact on the outcome of the consultation case. Students share the implementation process, evaluation of the intervention, and closure with the consultee. And, finally, the novice consultants identify the specific diversity issues that they perceived as part of the case as well as the lessons learned. The cases varied in their success of implementing an intervention with fidelity that resulted in positive outcomes. While some aspect of diversity existed in all cases, it was not necessarily the major reason interventions were not successful. One issue that also exists with many teachers is the lack of experience they have with the implementation of interventions. While they volunteered and were aware of the requirements as a consultee (e.g., they would be carrying out the intervention, not the consultant), some of them struggled with the process, partly due to their lack of experience implementing evidence-based interventions.

Each premise of the cases is in one of three categories: (a) consultation with teachers who present barriers, (b) consultation within the cultural context of poverty and race, and (c) culturally competent consultation practice that leads to success.

Consultation With Teachers Who Present Barriers

Chapter 3 is a case study about a teacher who acknowledged that he had difficulty connecting with his culturally diverse students and struggled with classroom management. This lack of understanding within this cultural context challenged both the consultation process as well as the successful implementation of the intervention.

Chapter 4 is a consultation case that evolves from the school's problem-solving team. While the process for the problem-solving team is to pair the teacher with a consultant to develop the intervention, the teacher is resistant to the help. The teacher's resistance and diversity issues in the school from a systems perspective are explored. Unlike the other cases, the consultant in the case was a doctoral intern placed in an urban school district. However, she was still considered a novice consultant, given that this was one of her first cases on internship.

Chapter 5 describes a case with a consultee who is culturally similar to her students but who appears to struggle to connect with them and has difficulty carrying out the intervention with integrity.

Consultation Within the Cultural Context of Poverty, Race, and School

Chapter 6 focuses on a teacher who is new to a school, grade level, and subject matter who attempts to connect with her students and recognizes that she may need diversity training to assist her in this effort.

Chapter 7 is a case study that presents two teachers who partner to carry out the same intervention. The consultants compare and contrast the consultation process with their respective teachers and work to understand the problem behaviors of the students in the cultural context of their environment both in the school as well as outside it.

Chapter 8 presents a case study that has multiple factors of diversity that potentially impact the case. The chapter outlines how the consultant attempts to understand those issues and work through them to meet the needs of the student.

Culturally Competent Consultation Practice Leads to Success

Chapters 9, 10, and 11 all describe working with culturally competent teachers who understand their students in a cultural context, adapt their teaching style to meet students' needs, demonstrate good classroom management, and have positive relationships with their students. Each of these interventions had positive outcomes.

Final Thoughts

Each consultant in these cases attempted to examine the case through a multicultural lens using both the ecological model and the MSC framework. While being a novice consultant learning the consultation process is challenging enough, adding in the MSC framework can be formidable. But learning and applying these simultaneously encourages the likelihood that this will become a part of their practice when they become a school psychologist and/or consultant. Having a diversity class that focused on awareness and knowledge was beneficial for the consultants to explore issues of diversity on multiple levels as well as recognize which issues might have an impact. In addition, they had to also learn to tease out whether knowledge about an issue of diversity gleaned from the research was actually the issue in some cases. While knowing the research on a variety of topics on diversity in education is essential, it is equally important to be able to apply the information appropriately and assess the accuracy for a particular case. The greatest challenge is not portraying the students, parents, and community as "victims" of their culture or to engage in "deficit theorizing." Authors share a narrative about their cases from their perspective, and it is truly the convergence of theory and practice.

The cases can be messy; they are certainly not perfect—but that is the point. These are learning experiences in which novice consultants reflect on real cases that are humanizing and reflective of the lived reality of a consultant in a diverse setting. It is hoped that this case study book will assist future and current consultants by reading these cases, using the questions both at the beginning and end of the chapters as reflection for how they would approach such a case, and being able to use the MSC framework when consulting about culturally diverse students and/or in culturally diverse environments.

References

Bandura, A. (1986). *Social foundations of thought and action: A social cognitive theory.* Englewood Cliffs, NJ: Prentice-Hall.

Bronfenbrenner, U. (1989). Ecological systems theory. *Annals of Child Development, 6,* 982–1022.

Erchul, W., & Young, H. L. (2014). Best practices in school consultation. In P. L. Harrison & A. Thomas (Eds.), *Best practices in school psychology: Data-based collaborative decision making* (pp. 449–460). Bethesda, MD: National Association of School Psychologists.

Gibbs, J. T. (1980). The interpersonal orientation in mental health consultation: Toward a model of ethnic variations in consultation. *Journal of Community Psychology, 8,* 195–207.

Ingraham, C. L. (2000). Consultation through a multicultural lens: Multicultural and cross-cultural consultation in schools. *School Psychology Review, 29,* 320–343.

Ingraham, C. L. (2003). Multicultural school consultation: When novice consultants explore cultural hypotheses with experienced teacher consultees. *School Psychology Review, 14,* 329–362.

Newell, M. L., Newell, T. S., & Looser, J. A. (2013). Examining how novice consultants address cultural factors during consultation: Illustration of a computer-simulated case-study method. *Consulting Psychology Journal: Practice and Research, 65,* 74–86.

Newman, D. (2012). Supervision of school-based consultation training: Addressing the concerns of novice consultants. In S. Rosenfield (Ed.), *Becoming a school consultant: Lessons learned* (pp. 49–70). New York, NY: Routledge.

Pinto, R. F. (1981). Consultant orientations and client system perception: Styles of cross-cultural consultation. In R. Lippitt & G. Lippit (Eds.), *Systems thinking: A resource for organization diagnosis and intervention* (pp. 57–114). Washington, DC: International Consultants Foundation.

Rogers, M. R. (2000). Examining the cultural context of consultation. *School Psychology Review, 29,* 414–415.

Rosenfield, S. (2012). Introduction: Becoming a school consultant. In S. Rosenfield (Ed.), *Becoming a school consultant: Lessons learned* (pp. 1–22). New York, NY: Routledge.

Sheridan, S. M. (2000). Considerations of multiculturalism and diversity in behavioral consultation with parents and teachers. *School Psychology Review, 29,* 344–353.

Zins, J. E., & Erchul, W. P. (2002). Best practices in school consultation. In A. Thomas & J. Grimes (Eds.), *Best practices in school psychology* (4th ed., pp. 625–643). Bethesda, MD: National Association of School Psychologists.

PART I

The Cultural Context of Schools

1

CONSULTING WITH A SOCIAL JUSTICE MIND-SET

Antoinette Halsell Miranda and Kisha M. Radliff

> The opposite of poverty is not wealth. In too many places, the opposite of poverty is justice.
>
> —Bryan Stevenson

Social justice is a term that can be abstract and difficult to define. It is a term that is complex in nature, especially when attempting to identify ways to put social justice into action. In its broadest sense, social justice is about ensuring equal access to liberties, rights, and opportunities in society. In education, social justice is increasingly being discussed given the inequities that exist for the most marginalized populations in American schools. Educators, researchers, and legislators have struggled to find and implement solutions that will close the achievement gap and level the playing field for all students to have a quality education that will lead to them being "college and career ready" after high school. However, far too many of our most vulnerable students continue to fall through the cracks. These students are disproportionately students of color and/or low income. Many of our "solutions" have focused on students at the individual level, with little acknowledgement of the broader societal issues that negatively impact students' academic achievement, social and emotional learning, and behavior. Most often, students are viewed as "victims" of their circumstances or, worse, complicit in creating their negative circumstances. In other words, we have too often engaged in "blaming the victim" for the poor outcomes that these students experience. As a society, what we have not been willing to do on a larger scale is address the broader societal issues that contribute to students' poor outcomes, such as poverty. In the past decade, however, increasing focus has been centered on examining the inequities in education as a social justice issue with a call to action. For example, increasing attention has been focused on the disproportionality of African American and Latino males being suspended and expelled from schools and how this contributes to the "school to prison" pipeline. This phenomenon has been framed as a social justice issue that requires an examination of the problem from a systems level. Looking at it from a systems level increases the chances that solutions will be implemented that impact a broader range of students and not just one individual at a time. Viewing educational challenges from a social justice perspective lends itself to examining how societal inequities, school culture, and the cultural context in which students exist contribute to or impact academic achievement and/or behavioral concerns. Education practitioners have an opportunity to embrace practicing in a socially just manner to address the inequities that exist and provide solutions to long-standing problems.

School-Based Consultants

School-based consultants (SBCs) have an opportunity to be a part of the solution. Unfortunately, there is not a plethora of research in the consultation literature on the social justice component that can guide consultants in what is best practice. Sander (2013), in her literature search for social justice–focused consultation articles, found 38 publications in the PsychINFO database. While there were a sparse number of articles, she did identify several areas that were important components in training consultants from a social justice lens. These included understanding the role of power and privilege and that consultants are in key positions to provide access to resources and power within school systems (Sander, 2013). While social justice is not often directly connected to consultation per se via the literature, it is becoming more prominent in the organizations that represent SBCs.

SBCs belong to a number of different professions (e.g., school psychologists, social workers, school counselors, and counseling psychologists) that have embraced social justice as part of their identity and have written about it for well over a decade. Social work describes social justice as their value system (National Association of Social Workers [NASW], n.d.). The NASW has long held the belief that social workers apply social justice principles to structural problems they encounter. Social justice was included in its code of ethics as one of its core values in 1996 and again in 2008. The NASW also views social justice as everyone deserving equal economic, political, and social rights and opportunities (NASW, n.d.).

Kiselica and Robinson (2001) articulate the historical foundation of social justice advocacy in counseling as well as events that advanced the social justice counseling perspective. In counseling, social justice is viewed as a multifaceted approach that embraces four critical principles: equity, access, participation, and harmony. The American Counseling Association has advocacy competencies that are considered a social justice framework for counselors (Ratts, Toporek, & Lewis, 2010).

School counselors are trained to view themselves as change agents. Bemak (2000) suggested that school counselors should embrace a social justice approach to deal with the countless needs of the students and families they serve. Griffin and Steen (2011) articulate what social justice within the context of the role of a school counselor would look like by suggesting strategies that could be used, as well as barriers to anticipate. The American School Counseling Association further supports the ideal of social justice through competencies that promote advocacy for marginalized groups that are consistent with the social justice framework. And, finally, the National Association of School Counselors has actively identified and promoted advocacy as a major aspect of school counselors' professional identities (Trusty & Brown, 2005).

In 2008, the *Journal of Educational and Psychological Consultation* published a thematic issue entitled "School Consultants as Agents of Social Justice." Commentators Speight and Vera (2009) rightly assessed that school psychology is just beginning to have discussions in the area of social justice, unlike the fields of counseling psychology and social work, which have been engaged in these issues much longer. They note that the four articles presented in the special issue did not define social justice, nor was there a common agreement about social justice across the articles. One of their suggestions was that school psychology needs to determine the meaning and relevance of social justice to the field.

Since that special issue, social justice has indeed become more prominent in the school psychology literature, as well as at conferences and through various statements from both the National Association of School Psychologists (NASP) and the American Psychological Association, Division 16, the organizations that represent the discipline. Shriberg et al. (2008) were instrumental in providing the first empirical study in which they conducted a Delphi study with 17 diversity experts in the field of school psychology who eventually defined social justice as "protecting the rights and opportunities for all" (p. 464). It was this seminal research that inspired the field to begin addressing social justice through special journal issues, an interest group in the NASP, and presentations at national conferences on social justice. In 2011 (Shriberg et al., 2011), a follow-up study was conducted with 1,000 randomly selected NASP members to determine their opinions on social justice as part of school psychology. Respondents ($N = 214$) rated *ensuring the protection of educational rights and opportunities* and *promoting nondiscriminatory practice* more important to the definition than any other element. In 2013, Shriberg, Song, Miranda, and Radliff edited the first book on social justice in school psychology that provided a vision for socially just school psychology practice in three different areas: (a) foundations, (b) major issues that affect practice, and (c) roles and functions of school psychologists. More than anything, the authors sought to encourage readers of the book to view *social justice* as a verb, something that we *do*, in advancing our work as advocates for the most disenfranchised group of children.

While school psychology has made great strides, in some ways we are still at the aspirational stage. Speight and Vera (2009) challenge us as a field to engage in critical self-analysis that would potentially "uncover the indirect, direct, and inadvertent ways that school psychology has supported the status quo and colluded with oppression" (p. 87). They rightly surmise that practitioners may end up reinforcing oppression because they are inside the system and therefore are unable to see the flaws and render a critique of that system. In some ways, school psychology is at a crossroads. We have written about the definition of social justice in terms of how school psychologists view it, identified programs that are training in this area, and written about how it might look in practice. But the real crux of a profession embracing the concept is the advancement of a social justice agenda with an action plan (Speight & Vera, 2009).

While many national organizations in which SBCs belong appear to have embraced the ideals of social justice, it doesn't necessarily correlate to consistent practice in the field that could be described as being from a social justice perspective. The need for a *social justice mind-set* when working in schools is evident when we acknowledge the complex societal issues that negatively impact students in K–12 schools, particularly those students residing in high-poverty communities. It has been well documented that issues in the environment as well as issues within the school context can negatively affect student outcomes (Children's Defense Fund, 2014). Students who live in poverty and/or are racially or ethnically diverse are the most vulnerable and have some of the most negative academic outcomes. While solutions have been proposed and implemented (e.g., No Child Left Behind), wide-sweeping improvements have yet to be seen. This is in part because we have used schools as our "playground" to effect change through education reform rather than examine social injustices within the school context, institutionalized oppression, broader policy issues, and societal factors that have been detrimental to the academic success of so many marginalized students. There is no doubt that the many helping professions understand the challenges that exist, but this does not necessarily translate to socially just practice. What are the barriers that prevent education professionals from viewing social justice as an aspirational goal to practicing with a social justice mind-set? While there are a number of potential barriers, one of the foremost barriers is the lack of training using a social justice framework. Three areas that should potentially be a part of preservice training are multicultural awareness, systems perspective, and advocacy.

Multicultural Awareness

Social justice and multiculturalism are often used interchangeably. The mission of social justice takes a broader stance than that of multiculturalism, and the goals of social justice cannot be addressed by multiculturalism alone (Bulhan, 1985). Although not always explicit, social justice has been the aim of those working to promote and develop multicultural competencies (Arredondo & Perez, 2003). An understanding and appreciation for multiculturalism is foundational to engaging in socially just practice. SBCs should, at a minimum, understand their own culture, the impact of their culture on others, respect and value other cultures, understand individual differences within cultural groups and multiple identities, and understand cultural saliency and how to build bridges (Ingraham, 2000). It will require training programs to be committed to providing a foundation in multiculturalism that leads to students developing a multicultural self-awareness as well as cultural competencies and advocacy competencies. An equally important aspect of multicultural training is understanding how bias, power, and privilege can limit success and foster discrimination and disempowerment of teachers, students, and/or parents within a system (Sue, 2008). Diversity or multicultural training enables the consultant to view situations through a multicultural lens. Oftentimes, the consultant is in a position to influence both teachers and administrators in terms of how they respond to situations and develop solutions that meet the needs of the child. As suggested by Williams and Greenleaf (2012), to move toward socially just solutions will require SBCs to examine environmental factors that impede the optimal development of students and to understand the complex interplay between individuals and their environments.

Systems Perspective

Most SBCs are trained to provide direct or indirect service at the individual level. Unfortunately, the many academic and behavior problems evident in low-income schools in particular require change at a systems level. The many societal issues that impact and influence K–12 students in a negative fashion have been well researched. The most notable are issues of poverty, racial or ethnic discrimination, unemployment, community violence, less qualified teachers, and food security, to name a few (Children's Defense Fund, 2014; Coleman-Jensen, Gregory, & Singh, 2014; Noguera, 2003; Wirt et al., 2004). In addition, there are school-based factors that can negatively impact student outcomes. These include but are not limited to school policies and practices, school culture, funding, teacher–student ratios, and qualified teaching staff (Noguera, 2003).

The various societal issues and school-based factors that negatively impact youth in schools require that SBCs engage in work at the systems level to effectively address the problems that the youth they serve experience. Further, systemic issues (e.g., referral bias, overidentification of racial and ethnic minorities) that contribute to the academic and behavioral concerns affecting youth must be considered to effectively engage in socially just practice. This would apply both at the systems level (e.g., examining practices that lead to referral biases of African American males) and the individual level (e.g., considering ecological factors that contribute to current behavioral concerns). Training that emphasizes a systems perspective as an integral aspect of the roles and responsibilities of SBCs is critical to providing a foundation for SBCs to build upon in practice. Specifically, training should extend beyond service at the individual level to teaching SBCs how to engage in service and advocacy at the systems level. For example, SBCs should be taught how to gather district- or school-level data to determine if unjust practices are occurring (e.g., overreferral of ethnic minorities for behavioral infractions) and provide guidance on how to use the data to advocate for all youth (e.g., to develop a standardized referral process that includes detailed information about what has been tried to address the behaviors). Additionally, systems-level data can be used at the individual level when an ecological framework is applied in practice. An ecological framework requires that the child be viewed within the context of the many environments in which he or she exists (e.g., home, school, peer groups, community). Thus, systems-level data contribute to a more comprehensive view of the problem. LaTosch and Jones (2012) discuss the challenge for social work students wanting to engage in macrolevel work in their field-based placements, which often have social workers and social work supervisors who were not formally trained in macrolevel work. Further complicating matters is the fact that core competencies in social work tend to be focused on microlevel-type tasks. This "dilemma" is probably similar in other school-based consultation field-based practicums as well as in practice.

Consulting with a social justice mind-set requires SBCs to use an ecological perspective that "explains human behavior as a function of person–environment interaction, thus providing [SBCs] with a philosophical rationale to engage in social action" (Williams & Greenleaf, 2012, p. 143). Williams and Greenleaf (2012) do an excellent job of laying out the needs for a "new discourse" for dealing effectively with student problems. It is an ecological discourse that "conceptualizes behavior as a result of intrapersonal qualities interacting with objects and systems in the environment" (Williams & Greenfield, 2012, p. 147). Thus, instead of always seeing problems as residing within the child, SBCs would also identify environmental factors that may contribute to the child's struggles and challenges. Williams and Greenfield (2012) view the ecological perspective as a contextual map that helps SBCs understand an individual's challenges within a broader social and cultural context. It is also hoped that an ecological approach will be the impetus for making changes within the system that will ultimately benefit a larger number of students.

Advocacy

Social justice as a *verb* requires SBCs to engage in advocacy. Helping profession organizations all have language that speaks to the advocacy nature of the work that they engage in to meet the needs of youth in schools. While organizations embrace advocacy and articulate the principles of advocacy, there is often a void in how advocacy becomes actualized in practice. Trusty and Brown (2005) attempt to address this void by articulating not only advocacy competencies for school counselors but also by taking it a step farther by providing a structure, purpose, and process for advocacy in school counselors' practice.

It is important to acknowledge that social justice advocacy, while noteworthy and necessary, is not an easy endeavor. It is critical that individuals are knowledgeable and feel empowered to engage as social justice advocates. Bemak and Chung (2005) provide some guidelines for engaging in social justice advocacy in school settings; these guidelines could be integrated at the training level or navigated at the point of independent practice. The goal of these guidelines is to enhance the SBC's knowledge of social justice and social injustices and to empower SBCs to engage in social justice advocacy. While these guidelines were written specifically for school counselors, they are easily adapted for other SBCs (Williams & Greenleaf, 2012). What follows is a brief overview of some of the most relevant guidelines to practice that Bemak and Chung propose for advocacy work (please see Bemak & Chung, 2005, for a detailed review).

- It is important to "view one's role as contributing to educational success for all students" (p. 200). By extension, this means that the practices an SBC engages in are consistent with this goal.
- SBCs should "emphasize social and educational equity and equal opportunity for all students" (p. 200). This extends to the consultative relationship in ensuring that all students are receiving equal and fair treatment and are receiving the support and resources that they need and that the SBC advocates for all youth.
- Given the often limited time that SBCs have, working in groups can be beneficial to meet the needs of more youth and educators. This could be particularly beneficial when there are overlapping concerns for multiple students within a classroom or a grade level, for example.
- Engage youth and parents in a collaborative partnership. Foster empowerment by providing them with knowledge about their rights and the tools to advocate for themselves. This has the potential to build a stronger school community and to address broader social injustices.
- Attempting to create systemic change in isolation can be challenging, if not nearly impossible. SBCs should develop relationships with key personnel who are integral to creating lasting systemic change (e.g., principals, administrators). Develop allies within the system.
- Connected to the previous point, SBCs should forge collaborative relationships with other SBCs within the school and/or school district. This can be particularly beneficial for identifying social injustices occurring across the district. Data provided from a school- or district-wide level can be a powerful tool to initiating change. Further, the collaboration among SBCs creates a larger voice that can be more powerful in creating systemic change.

These are various suggestions that SBCs can integrate into their practice to further their knowledge and engage in social justice advocacy. As is evident from this list, many of these suggestions involve the use of data (across the individual and systems level); empowerment of others, students, and their families in particular; and collaboration with key personnel and other SBCs to engage in advocacy to more effectively address social justice issues.

A Social Justice Mind-Set

In the past decade, the term *social justice* has increasingly become part of the vernacular of helping professions. While we've known for decades that certain groups are disenfranchised, marginalized, and othered, especially in the educational system, it is only recently that we are discussing these impactful inequities in education as a social justice issue with a call, at least by professional organizations, to become change agents and embrace a social justice framework. The challenge is translating an aspirational goal into practice. While the SBCs' professional organizations have embraced the concept through standards, white papers, and competencies, to name a few, it doesn't necessarily mean that this has translated to what is occurring in practice. For this to happen, preservice training is critical in preparing SBCs to embrace socially just practices. While there can be hope that practicing practitioners will embrace a social justice agenda, preservice training is more likely to have an influence on the future practitioner emerging with a social justice mind-set. Griffin and Steen (2011) discuss barriers and challenges to social justice advocacy identified by school counselors, such as lack of funding for necessary resources, minimal knowledge of cultural differences, and fear of confronting the status quo, to name a few. They suggest action items to combat the achievement gap but acknowledge that first and foremost, preservice school counselors and those in the field "will need to intentionally engage in social-justice collaborative advocacy work to make the greatest impact on their schools and surrounding communities" (p. 82–83). We would agree that this is true for all SBCs who are truly committed to becoming social justice change agents for the purpose of transforming schools.

Social justice practice can begin by embracing CARE: cultural competency, advocacy, relationship building, and empowering and engaging. Each of these is minimally necessary to begin to effect change both at an individual and a systems level when embracing socially just practice. Cultural competency is necessary in order to be knowledgeable as well as to understand the diverse populations that SBCs will be working with. In addition, it is vital that SBCs know and understand societal issues as well as the cultural context in which students exist. Advocacy requires SBCs to be bold and persistent when speaking up and out for those most marginalized in the educational system. Relationship building is critical, as SBCs seek to collaborate with various stakeholders to make system changes at both the macro- and microlevels. And, finally, SBCs should work to empower and engage parents, students, teachers, and other stakeholders to be a part of school transformation. Educational inequities of our most marginalized students in our public schools are our greatest challenge and our greatest tragedy. SBCs are in a position to challenge the status quo, which requires courage and conviction.

References

Arredondo, P., & Perez, P. (2003). Expanding multicultural competence through social justice leadership. *The Counseling Psychologist, 31*, 282–289. http://dx.doi.org/10.1177/0011000003031003003

Bemak, F. (2000). Transforming the role of the counselor to provide leadership in educational reform through collaboration. *Professional School Counseling, 3*(5), 323–331.

Bemak, F., & Chung, R.C.Y. (2005). Advocacy as a critical role for urban school counselors: Working toward equity and social justice. *Professional School Counseling, 8*, 196–202.

Bulhan, H.A. (1985). *Frantz Fanon and the psychology of oppression.* New York, NY: Plenum.

Children's Defense Fund. (2014). *The state of America's children.* Washington, DC. Retrieved February 10, 2015, from http://www.childrensdefense.org/library/state-of-americas-children/2014-soac.pdf

Coleman-Jensen, A., Gregory, C., & Singh, A. (2014). *Household food security in the United States in 2013* (Staff Report No. ERR-173). Washington, DC: Economic Research Service, United States Department of Agriculture (USDA).

Griffin, D., & Steen, S. (2011). A social justice approach to school counseling. *Journal for Social Action in Counseling and Psychology, 3*, 74–85.

Ingraham, C. L. (2000). Consultation through a multicultural lens: Multicultural and cross-cultural consultation in schools. *School Psychology Review, 29*, 320–343.

Kiselica, M.S., & Robinson, M. (2001). Bringing advocacy counseling to life: The history, issues, and human dramas of social justice work in counseling. *Journal of Counseling & Development, 79*, 387–397.

LaTosch, K., & Jones, K. (2012). Conducting macro-level work in a micro-focused profession. *Practice Digest, 2.1*, 1–3.

National Association of Social Workers (NASW). (n.d.). Social justice. Retrieved April 13, 20015, from http://socialworkers.org/pressroom/features/issue/peace.asp

Noguera, P. A. (2003). *City schools and the American dream: Reclaiming the promise of public education.* New York, NY: Teachers College Press.

Ratts, M. J., Toporek, R., & Lewis, J. A. (2010). *ACA advocacy competencies: A social justice framework for counselors.* Alexandria, VA: American Counseling Association.

Sander, J. (2013). Consultation and collaboration. In D. Shriberg., S. Song, A.H. Miranda, & K.M. Radliff (Eds.), *School psychology and social justice* (pp. 225–243). New York, NY: Routledge.

Shriberg, D., Bonner, M., Sarr, B.J., Walker, A.M., Hyland, M., & Chester, C. (2008). Social justice through a school psychology lens: Definition and applications. *School Psychology Review, 37*, 453–468.

Shriberg, D., Song, S.Y., Miranda, A.H., & Radliff, K.M. (2013). *School psychology and social justice: Conceptual foundations and tools for practice.* New York, NY: Routledge.

Shriberg, D., Wynee, E., Briggs, A., Bartucci, G., & Lombardo, A. (2011). School psychologists' perspectives on social justice. *School Psychology Forum: Research in Practice, 5*, 37–53.

Speight, S.L., & Vera, E.M. (2009). The challenge of social justice for school psychology. *Journal of Educational and Psychological Consultation, 19*, 82–92.

Sue, D.W. (2008). Multicultural organizational consultation: A social justice perspective. *Consulting Psychology Journal: Practice and Research, 60,* 157–169.

Trusty, J., & Brown, D. (2005). Advocacy competencies for professional school counselors. *Professional School Counseling, 8,* 259–266.

Williams, J.M., & Greenleaf, A.T. (2012). Ecological psychology: Potential contributions to social justice and advocacy in school settings. *Journal of Educational and Psychological Consultation, 22,* 141–157.

Wirt, J., Rooney, P., Choy, S., Provasnik, S., Sen, A., & Tobin, R. (2004). *The condition of education 2004* (NCES 2004–077). Washington, DC: National Center for Educational Statistics, Institute of Education Sciences. Retrieved April 10, 2015, from http://nces. ed.gov/pubsearch/pubsinfo.asp?pubid=2004077

2

ENGAGING IN CULTURALLY RESPONSIVE CONSULTATION PRACTICES

Emilia C. Lopez and Jennifer Kong

Consultation is an indirect problem-solving process in which consultants, such as school psychologists or other support personnel, collaborate with consultees to address concerns about students' academic, behavioral, and mental health difficulties (Brown, Pryzwansky, & Schulte, 2001). Research evidence shows strong support for the behavioral, instructional, and conjoint models of consultation in terms of client (i.e., improved instructional and behavioral outcomes) and consultee outcomes (i.e., change in teacher and parent behaviors and in their conceptualization of the consultation referral problem; Lopez & Nastasi, 2014). The literature and research also point to essential process components of effective consultation such as effective communication and collaborative practices. Culturally responsive practices have also been identified as pivotal in delivering consultation.

Using a wide consultation lens, culturally responsive practices involve addressing the interactions of cultural, ethnic, race, language, religion, gender, and disability variables in the context of consultation processes such as communicating, collaborating, and building rapport with consultees. Consultee-centered approaches that are culturally responsive guide consultants while they support consultees to examine their perceptions of culturally diverse clients and the strategies they can utilize to address issues of diversity. Problem-solving methods used in culturally responsive consultation are sensitive to cultural differences and include using appropriate tools to identify the problem in consultation and planning and implementing interventions that are culturally appropriate. Evaluating consultation processes and outcomes within a culturally responsive framework also involves careful attention to the examination of processes used in consultation (e.g., Were effective cross-cultural communication skills used when interacting with the consultee?) and achieved outcomes (e.g., change in consultee's confidence in working with a culturally diverse student, change in instructional outcomes for an English-language learner using instructional consultation).

Building a Framework for Culturally Responsive Consultation

As early as the 1970s, Westermeyer and Hausman (1974) rendered a call for consultants to incorporate multicultural strategies within their consultation practices. In the following decade, Gibbs (1985) argued for the need to prepare consultants to address multicultural issues in consultation using didactic, fieldwork, and supervision experiences. The 1990s were a prolific decade for multicultural consultation, as experts in the field began to more clearly conceptualize major components of practice and training (e.g., Brown, 1997; Jackson & Hayes, 1993; Ramirez, Lepage, Kratochwill, & Duffy, 1998). It was during that decade that Tarver Behring and Ingraham (1998) defined multicultural consultation as a culturally sensitive, indirect service process in which the consultant adjusts the consultation services to address the needs and cultural values of the consultee and the client.

Ingraham (2000) advanced the literature and practice of consultation by developing the multicultural and cross-cultural consultation framework in school psychology. According to Ingraham (2004), multicultural consultation "considers the potential influence of culture on the consultation process and the individuals involved in the consultation triad" (p. 135). This framework has a wide utility because it can be incorporated into any of the major consultation models (e.g., behavioral, instructional, conjoint, mental health). Ingraham (2004) broadly defines culture as "an organized set of thoughts, beliefs, and norms for interaction and communication," and cross-cultural issues are addressed as consultants work with consultees across cultures (p. 325). Ingraham's (2000) framework guides consultants as they support consultees to increase their knowledge, skills, confidence, and objectivity around multicultural issues. Among the methods consultants use to support consultees are supporting cross-cultural learning and motivation, modeling for consultees as they acquire multicultural skills, and communicating using culturally sensitive strategies.

Across the literature in culturally responsive consultation, there are several major underlying principles that frame the practice and training of consultation (Lopez & Truesdell, 2007). One major principle is that consultants are sensitive to cultural differences, show awareness of such differences, and develop an awareness of their own attitudes and beliefs in order to understand how their own perceptions impact the consultation process. In order for consultation to be effective, consultants and consultees also strive toward learning about their consultees' and clients' cultural backgrounds (as cultural awareness and knowledge guide how we relate with consultees), understanding the clients' difficulties, and engaging in problem solving during consultation. Since communication and personal interactions are central to consultation, consultants are attentive to cultural differences during communicative interactions and must be mindful of verbal and nonverbal communication patterns in cross-cultural situations. As a process, consultants acknowledge that their backgrounds, beliefs, and attitudes impact their relationships with consultees and play a part in rapport building, interpersonal interactions, and collaborative efforts. In a culturally responsive consultation framework, multicultural issues are addressed in every stage of the consultation process, including contracting, relationship building, problem identification and analysis, intervention planning and implementation, and evaluation. Finally, a major underlying principle in culturally responsive consultation is that consultants also acknowledge and address systemic issues such as organizational practices and policies that impact consultants, consultees, and clients. These underlying principles are directly linked to process and outcome issues in consultation and are reflected in the existing research addressing culturally responsive practices.

Research in Culturally Responsive Consultation Practices

The research in multicultural consultation supports the idea that engaging in culturally responsive practices impacts process as well as outcomes in consultation. Gibbs (1980) investigated relationship building in consultation between Black consultants and Black and White teacher consultees in an urban school district. He found that Black consultees preferred an interpersonal consultation style that focused on the process, while White consultees preferred an instrumental communication style that was goal or task oriented. Gibbs (1980) suggested that Blacks are more likely than Whites to initially focus more on interpersonal aspects of consultation due to a combination of historical circumstances and sociocultural patterns and values. He concluded that cultural and racial group membership influenced consultees' expectations and preferences during consultation and argued that consultants need to adjust their interpersonal styles when communicating with consultees of diverse racial backgrounds.

Duncan and Pryzwansky (1993) also investigated the impact of racial variables on consultation processes. The investigators asked a sample of Black female elementary school teachers to watch videotapes of consultation sessions and then provide their perceptions of the consultants' effectiveness. The study found that the consultees' ratings of the consultants' effectiveness did not differ significantly as a function of the consultants' race. In addition, the teachers did not report preferences regarding the consultants' racial backgrounds. In a qualitative analysis of the findings, several participants reported that the quality of the help given was more important than the consultants' race.

Rogers (1998) reported similar findings as Duncan and Pryzwansky (1993) when exploring the relationship between race and consultants' perceived competency by showing a videotape of a consultation session to 154 African American and Caucasian female preservice teachers. The study reported that, regardless of the consultants' race, teachers rated consultants who addressed racial themes as more competent and as more culturally sensitive compared to those consultants who ignored racial issues.

The most critical implication of these studies is that consultants who address cultural issues in consultation are perceived as more effective and competent by consultees. Thus, the consultants' multicultural knowledge and skills are important when engaging in consultation.

Several qualitative studies in consultation have documented the impact of culturally responsive practices on consultation processes and outcomes. Goldstein and Harris (2000) explored the implications of using a multicultural consultation approach in two heterogeneous schools with a Latino population. The investigators interviewed Latino parents from two schools and found that they differed in terms of their formal educational experiences in their native country and their reasons for migration (e.g., political turbulence, socioeconomic opportunities, escape from strict class boundaries). The variation of experiences impacted parents' perceptions of how their children should be instructed to learn English. Parents in one school wanted their children to be instructed solely in English and viewed bilingual education as an instructional program that deterred their children from learning English. In contrast, parents in the second school wanted their children to have access to bilingual education and perceived bilingual instruction as a medium to maintain their children's native culture and language.

Perceptions of how instruction should be delivered also became a focus of consultation in Goldstein and Harris' (2000) study, as parents and school professionals had their own perceptions and expectations of how the students should be instructed. The researchers described how consultants had to clearly communicate with both parents and school staff in order to understand their differences and commonalities. Much of their communication entailed discussing their attitudes toward programs such as bilingual education, bilingual special education, and effective instruction for English-language learners. The consultants explored within-group differences in the Latino community reflecting divergent approaches as to how to instruct students to learn English as a second language. The consultants reported relying on different strategies in each school to bridge the gap between the parents and school staff. In the school in which the parents did not want bilingual education, the consultants conducted meetings for parents to address their concerns, provided information regarding learning disabilities and special education instruction, and coordinated meetings with other bilingual special education staff at various schools to share information with parents about various instructional approaches. In the school in which parents advocated for bilingual education services, the consultant helped train bilingual and special education paraprofessionals, disseminated instructional information, integrated services within bilingual classrooms, and adapted materials using bilingual education methodology. The investigators argued that it was imperative for consultants to demonstrate knowledge of cultural values and skills in addressing systemic issues. Furthermore, they concluded that it was necessary for consultants to examine and be aware of within-group cultural differences to appropriately and effectively apply multicultural frameworks.

The consultation research supports that consultants modify their consultation strategies when working with diverse populations. Tarver Behring, Cabello, Kushida, and Murguia (2000) investigated the kinds of modifications made to school-based consultation by interviewing beginning consultants of four different ethnic identities. Consultants of European American, African American, Asian American, and Latino backgrounds consulted with teachers and families of ethnically similar and different groups. Interviews with consultants (teachers) and clients (parents and students), who were either from the same or different cultural backgrounds as the consultants, revealed that consultants often made modifications to their consultation approaches in response to cultural diversity. The modifications included (a) discussing cultural issues with consultees, (b) respecting students' and parents' cultural styles, (c) allowing more time to move through the stages of consultation to explore cultural differences and issues, and (d) communicating in the parents' native language. In addition, consultants reported making different modifications for specific cultural groups. For example, in a case with a Latino family, consultants met with the family in their own neighborhood, communicated in Spanish, showed respect for and were responsive to specific Latino cultural customs, and suggested a school-sponsored literacy program in the community that included English-language instruction for both the student and the parent. In another case, the consultant working with an Asian family reported using strategies that were viewed as more responsive to Asian cultural values and attitudes, such as applying a more expert approach when discussing educational services with the parent, de-emphasizing the child's deficits to avoid family shame, avoiding personal questions, and accepting a gift of gratitude at the end of the case. According to Tarver Behring and Ingraham (1998), these findings suggest that using multicultural approaches does not only entail consultants making cultural modifications when working with consultees and clients from diverse backgrounds but also includes making culture-specific modifications to match the culture of the consultees and clients.

In a qualitative investigation, Ingraham (2003) found that the use of culturally responsive strategies impacted consultation outcomes. Ingraham (2003) examined how three novice consultants applied multicultural approaches to explore cultural hypotheses with experienced teachers as consultees. The results demonstrated that consultants in two successful cases used multicultural approaches such as self-disclosing regarding the consultant's own cultural learning process and experiences, reframing consultees' perceptions of cultural issues, bridging across differences by highlighting similarities between consultants and consultees of diverse backgrounds, creating emotional safety when addressing cultural and racial issues, coconstructing the definition of the consultation referral problem within a multicultural context, and reframing cultural perspectives.

In contrast, Ingraham (2000) reported that consultants who avoided addressing cultural issues (e.g., consultees' attitudes toward cultural differences) and who did not use multicultural strategies were not able to change consultees' perceptions or improve their relationships with the consultees to address issues such as differences in how students' difficulties were perceived (i.e., consultees viewing students' cultural differences as problems). The findings support the hypothesis that positive consultation outcomes are achieved when consultants address multicultural issues during the consultation process. The student outcomes in this qualitative investigation included increases in student participation, academic achievement, and targeted classroom behaviors. The consultee outcomes included increased consultee engagement in the process of problem solving and knowledge and skills in working with culturally and linguistically diverse students. Ingraham (2003) concluded that consultants need to develop specific knowledge and skills to address the range and intensity of cultural values and attitudes that they may encounter when delivering consultation within a multicultural framework.

In general, the studies reviewed above suggest that using culturally responsive approaches in consultation impact consultation processes and outcomes (Duncan & Pryzwansky, 1993; Goldstein & Harris, 2000; Ingraham, 2003; Rogers, 1998; Tarver Behring et al., 2000). These studies also suggest that multicultural approaches in consultation call for a variety of culturally responsive consultation competencies.

Culturally Responsive Consultation Competencies

Pivotal consultation skills have been identified in the literature, such as communication skills, collaborative problem solving, and personal characteristics that include maintaining rapport and demonstrating empathy (West & Cannon, 1998). The consultation literature also refers to a wide range of competencies in which school psychologists need to engage in culturally responsive consultation (e.g., Brown, 1997; Brown et al., 2001; Ingraham, 2000; Lopez & Rogers, 2001; Miller & Cangemi, 1988; Ramirez et al., 1998; Rogers & Lopez, 2002; Sheridan, 2000; Ton, Koike, Hales, Johnson, & Hilty, 2005; Washburn, Manley, & Holiwski, 2003).

Ingraham (2000) identified learning and development domains for consultants within her multicultural consultation framework. The domains include (a) understanding one's own culture, (b) understanding the impact of one's own culture on others, (c) respecting and valuing other cultures, (d) understanding individual differences within cultural groups and multiple identities, (e) using cross-cultural communication and multicultural consultation approaches for rapport development and maintenance, (f) understanding cultural saliency and how to build bridges across salient differences, (g) understanding the cultural context for consultation, and (h) using multicultural consultation and interventions appropriate for the consultees and clients.

There are only three sources in school psychology that have used empirical approaches to identify multicultural competencies. Lopez and Rogers (2001) and Rogers and Lopez (2002) used quantitative methodology via Delphi procedures to identify multicultural competencies across 14 major school psychology domains, roles, and functions that included consultation (e.g., assessment, language, professional characteristics, assessment, report writing). Rogers and Lopez (2002) reviewed the literature in multicultural school psychology, identified literature-based competencies, and then asked a panel of experts to rate and identify the most important competencies. The cross-cultural consultation competencies identified in that investigation were (a) knowledge about cultural and linguistic factors that can influence the input, process, and outcome of consultation; (b) skills to work with linguistically and culturally diverse parents, children, and school staff; (c) skills to use a variety of data collection techniques for problem identification, clarification, planning, and implementation of interventions that are culturally and linguistically sensitive; and (d) skills to recognize prejudice and prevalent obstacles that may affect consultation (e.g., racism, sexism).

Lopez and Rogers (2001) used a different approach to identify essential multicultural competencies by asking a panel of experts to first identify relevant consultation competencies and subsequently rate which were the most important. Four multicultural consultation competency items were rated as most important by the expert panel as follows: (a) skill in working with others (e.g., patience, good judgment), (b) skill in demonstrating sensitivity toward the culture of school personnel involved in consultation, (c) skill in responding flexibly with a range of possible solutions that reflect sensitivity to cross-cultural issues, and (d) knowledge of the culturally related factors that may affect accurate assessment of the "problem" in the problem-solving sequence. The two Delphi studies identified a total of eight essential multicultural competencies that were relevant to multicultural consultation. The competencies focused on knowledge and skills; they also reflected process- as well as outcome-related competencies.

In a recent investigation, Kong and Lopez (2011) surveyed the consultation literature and used systematic procedures to identify a total of 40 multicultural consultation competencies. The competencies identified were used to validate the Multicultural School-Based Consultation Competency Scale, which included awareness, knowledge, and skills in multicultural consultation. Among the multicultural competencies identified were (a) awareness of how consultees from diverse cultural and ethnic backgrounds may differ as to how they view the roles of consultants and consultants' own values and biases and how they may impact interactions with consultees; (b) knowledge of cross-cultural communication styles and how the consultants' own cultural backgrounds impact the consultation process; and (c) skills in demonstrating sensitivity toward the cultural backgrounds of school personnel involved in consultation, adopting a culturally responsive consultation style for more effective communication, designing intervention evaluation tools that are sensitive to cultural and language differences, using a variety of data collection techniques for problem identification and clarification that are culturally and linguistically sensitive, and identifying bias and prejudicial attitudes at the individual and organizational levels.

Similar to Lopez and Rogers (2001) and Rogers and Lopez (2002), the competencies identified by Kong and Lopez (2011) highlighted process and outcome components in consultation. These findings clearly imply that engaging in culturally responsive practices requires numerous essential competencies. Our attention must then be directed toward examining how to acquire pivotal multicultural competencies to engage in consultation.

Developing Culturally Responsive Consultation Competencies

The aforementioned consultation research has reached two general conclusions that provide a compelling rationale for clearly deliberating on the issue of how to prepare consultants to deliver culturally responsive consultation services. One general finding is that consultation must be embedded within multicultural practices in order to obtain effective outcomes since skills such as cross-cultural communication and using culturally sensitive problem-solving approaches directly impact consultation outcomes for clients and consultees. The other general finding in the consultation research is that there are essential multicultural consultation knowledge and skills that consultants must demonstrate to engage in culturally responsive practices.

Anton-LaHart and Rosenfield (2004) investigated the state of preservice consultation training and supervision in school psychology programs. The researchers found that most preservice training courses emphasized instruction focusing on consultation theory and content and provided less instruction about multicultural skills. Multicultural skills received little emphasis in consultation courses and were taught, on average, "between 0 and 10% of the time" (p. 49). The findings suggest that graduate training programs must allocate more time toward preparing future school psychologists to deliver culturally responsive consultation support.

Rosenfield, Levinsohn-Klyap, and Cramer (2010) provide a stage-driven developmental framework for the acquisition of competencies in consultation. The learners' stages advance from novice to expert level. During the acclimation stage, the consultants begin to acquire basic knowledge about consultation in terms of concepts and skills. This stage is followed by early competence, during which consultants continue to acquire additional skills by applying them to cases. Consultation fieldwork experiences are important for continued growth in consultation skills. Consultants who continue to receive supervision and support as learners are able to achieve full competence. The expert level is mastered when consultants engage in consultation and further develop their skills through continuing education opportunities.

Parallel frameworks exist for the development and teaching of cultural competence. Cross, Bazron, Dennis, and Isaacs (1989) developed the cultural competence continuum, which includes cultural destructiveness (i.e., cultural differences are not acknowledged and practices are destructive toward culturally diverse individuals or groups); cultural incapacity (i.e., cultural differences are ignored and the individual is unable to respond to cultural differences); cultural blindness (i.e., cultural differences are acknowledged but not recognized as pivotal); cultural precompetence (i.e., cultural differences are acknowledged and the individual is aware that there is room for growth); cultural competence (i.e., cultural differences are valued and practices demonstrate cultural knowledge); and cultural proficiency (i.e., cultural differences are consistently recognized and practices integrate cultural issues in meaningful ways).

An integration of these two developmental frameworks for the acquisition of competencies in culturally responsive consultation entails helping consultants to further develop their consultation skills while also incorporating multicultural awareness, knowledge, and skills. A major challenge facing our school psychology preparation programs is identifying the instructional strategies and tools that we can use to better equip novice consultants to deliver culturally responsive consultation services (Lopez & Rogers, 2010; Rosenfield et al., 2010). Practicing school psychologists also need to learn and develop those competencies, as some may have learned consultation but not within a culturally responsive framework. Courses and workshops in consultation are the didactic venues that are typically used to prepare school psychology graduate students and practitioners (Rosenfield et al., 2010). These training venues can incorporate many teaching methods such as lectures, group supervision, role plays, and case studies.

The chapters in this book provide a series of consultation case studies that are framed within culturally responsive practices. The authors reflect upon their challenges and accomplishments while providing us with important perspectives as to practices that are conducive to deliver consultation in multicultural situations. Pryzwansky and Noblit (1990) argued for the use of case studies as a valuable means to expand school psychologists' knowledge and skills about consultation. They described case studies as having "a unique strength of providing a format to understand the dynamics of a situation, linking context, processes, and outcomes" (p. 297).

Case studies are valuable resources within a culturally responsive framework to explore issues related to culture, language, religion, race, gender, and ethnicity and how they impact process and outcomes in consultation. Furthermore, case studies provide a vehicle for culturally responsive consultants to reflect upon their practices so that we as learners can all benefit from their insights. As a learning process, they encourage us to engage in self-reflection about our own values, attitudes, and actions as we engage in the consultation process using culturally responsive practices.

Conclusion

Delivering culturally responsive consultation services requires consultants to develop and demonstrate a wide range of competencies that emerge over time via training and practice. Culturally responsive practices in consultation require consultants to demonstrate awareness, knowledge, and skills that are embedded in a multicultural framework. This book is the first to compile a collection of case studies that offers us the opportunity to reflect upon how to engage in culturally responsive practices when engaging in consultation. As readers, we thank the authors for their reflections and for helping us to embark upon our own journey as culturally responsive consultants.

References

Anton-LaHart, J., & Rosenfield, S. (2004). A survey of preservice consultation training in school psychology programs. *Journal of Educational and Psychological Consultation, 15*, 41–62.

Brown, D. (1997). Implications of cultural values for cross-cultural consultation with families. *Journal of Counseling and Development, 76*, 29–35.

Brown, D., Pryzwansky, W.B., & Schulte, A.C. (2001). *Psychological consultation introduction to theory and practice* (5th ed.). Boston, MA: Allyn & Bacon.

Cross, T., Bazron, B., Dennis, K., & Isaacs, M. (1989). Towards a culturally competent system of care. Washington, DC: CASSP Technical Assistance Center, Georgetown University Child Development Center.

Duncan, C.F., & Pryzwansky, W.B. (1993). Effects of race, racial identity development, and orientation style on perceived consultant effectiveness. *Journal of Multicultural Counseling and Development, 21*, 88–96.

Gibbs, J.T. (1980). The interpersonal orientation in mental health consultation: Toward a model of ethnic variations in consultation. *Journal of Community Psychology, 8*, 195–207.

Gibbs, J.T. (1985). Can we continue to be color-blind and class-bound? *The Counseling Psychologist, 13*, 426–435.

Goldstein, B.S.C., & Harris, K.C. (2000). Consultant practices in two heterogeneous Latino schools. *School Psychology Review, 29*, 368–377.

Ingraham, C.L. (2000). Consultation through a multicultural lens: Multicultural and cross-cultural consultation in schools. *School Psychology Review, 29*, 320–343.

Ingraham, C.L. (2003). Multicultural consultee-centered consultation: When novice consultants explore cultural hypotheses with experienced teacher consultees. *Journal of Educational and Psychological Consultation, 14*, 329–362.

Ingraham, C.L. (2004). Consultee-centered consultation: Improving the quality of professional services in schools and community organizations. In N.M. Lambert, I. Hylander, & J.H. Sandoval (Eds.), *Multicultural consultee-centered consultation: Supporting consultees in the development of cultural competence* (pp. 133–148). Mahwah, NJ: Erlbaum.

Jackson, D.N., & Hayes, D.H. (1993). Multicultural issues in consultation. *Journal of Counseling and Development, 72*, 144–147.

Kong, J., & Lopez, E.C. (2011). *Development and validation of the Multicultural School-Based Consultation Competency Scale* (Doctoral dissertation). Available from ProQuest Dissertations and Theses database. (UMI No. 3481659)

Lopez, E.C., & Nastasi, B.K. (2014). Process and outcome research in selected models of consultation. In W.P. Erchul & S.M. Sheridan (Eds.), *Handbook of research in school consultation* (pp. 304–320). New York, NY: Routledge.

Lopez, E.C., & Rogers, M. (2010). Multicultural competence and diversity: University and field collaboration. In J. Kaufman, T.L. Hughes, & C.A. Riccio (Eds.), *Handbook* of education, training, and supervision of school psychologists in school and community. Volume II: Bridging the training and practice gap: Building cooperative university/field practices (pp. 111–128). Washington, DC: National Association of School Psychologists.

Lopez, E.C., & Rogers, M.R. (2001). Conceptualizing cross-cultural school psychology competencies. *School Psychology Quarterly, 16*, 270–302.

Lopez, E.C., & Truesdell, L. (2007). Multicultural issues in instructional consultation for English language learning students. In G.B. Esquivel, E.C. Lopez, & S.G. Nahari (Eds.), *Handbook of multicultural school psychology: An interdisciplinary perspective* (pp. 71–98). Mahwah, NJ: Erlbaum.

Miller, R.L., & Cangemi, J.P. (1988). Developing trust in international companies. *Organization Development Journal, 6*, 26–28.

Pryzwansky, W.B., & Noblit, G.W. (1990). Understanding and improving consultation practice: The qualitative case study approach. *Journal of Educational and Psychological Consultation, 1*, 293–307.

Ramirez, S.Z., Lepage, K.M., Kratochwill, T.R., & Duffy, J.L. (1998). Multicultural issues in school-based consultation: Conceptual and research considerations. *Journal of School Psychology, 36*, 479–509.

Rogers, M.R. (1998). The influence of race and consultant verbal behavior on perceptions of consultant competence and multicultural sensitivity. *School Psychology Quarterly, 13*, 265–280.

Rogers, M.R., & Lopez, E.C. (2002). Identifying critical cross-cultural school psychology competencies. *Journal of School Psychology, 40*, 115–141.

Rosenfield, S., Levinsohn-Klyap, M., & Cramer, K. (2010). Educating consultants for practice in the schools. In E. Garcia-Vasquez, T. Crespi, & C. Riccio (Eds.), *Handbook of education, training and supervision of school psychologists in school and community—Volume I: Foundations of professional practice* (pp. 259–278). New York, NY: Routledge.

Sheridan, S.M. (2000). Considerations of multiculturalism and diversity in behavioral consultation with parents and teachers. *School Psychology Review, 29*, 344–353.

Tarver Behring, S., Cabello, B., Kushida, D., & Murguia, A. (2000). Cultural modifications to current school-based consultation approaches reported by culturally diverse beginning consultants. *School Psychology Review, 29*, 354–367.

Tarver Behring, S., & Ingraham, C.L. (1998). Culture as a central component of consultation: A call to the profession. *Journal of Educational and Psychological Consultation, 9*, 57–72.

Ton, H., Koike, A., Hales, R.E., Johnson, J., & Hilty, D. (2005). A qualitative needs assessment for development of a cultural consultation service. *Transcultural Psychiatry, 42*, 491–504.

Washburn, J.J., Manley, T., & Holiwski, F. (2003). Teaching on racism: Tools for consultant training. *Journal of Educational and Psychological Consultation, 14*, 387–399.

West, J.F., & Cannon, G.S. (1988). Essential collaborative consultation competencies for regular and special educators. *Journal of Learning Disabilities, 21*, 56–63.

Westermeyer, J., & Hausman, W. (1974). Cross cultural consultation for mental health planning. *International Journal of Social Psychiatry, 20*(1–2), 34–38.

PART II

Consultation With Teachers Who Present Barriers

3

WHAT TO DO WHEN A CONSULTEE VIEWS STUDENTS AS THE PROBLEM

Erin M. McClure

Advance Organizer Questions

- What skills will the consultant need to utilize to provide effective consultation within a turbulent school culture?
- How can the teacher's perception of the problem behavior in the classroom shape his willingness to complete an intervention with integrity?
- What are some components of this case that must be addressed prior to the implementation of a successful intervention?

School Culture

Before school consultation begins, school culture and its potential impact on the relationship with the consultee must be considered by the consultant. Since schools are open systems and their barriers to the outside world are permeable by many external forces at the local, state, and national levels, it is important to recognize how these forces can influence the school climate and culture. In fact, "school consultation does not take place in a vacuum. The larger organizational context needs to be understood by the consultant in order to be an effective school-based consultant" (Rosenfield, 2012, p. 6). I found that by considering the factors found in Bronfenbrenner's "exosphere" (1989) at my practicum site, I was able to gain a more holistic systems perspective on the consultant–consultee relationship.

At my consultation placement, I spent an hour per week at an urban elementary school, where I worked to implement a classroom-wide behavioral intervention. Before starting at the school, my program coordinator provided my cohort with some background information on the building and school district and its current state of affairs. One concerning factor was that the teachers had already been informed that they would be let go at the conclusion of the school year. This termination—and the option for the principal to rehire up to 40% of the staff—was due to the school's state report card designation for the third consecutive year as an "academic emergency." Termed *reconstitution*, the process has been utilized within this large urban school system as a means of turning around the school with a new staff and, subsequently, a new culture.

Since this intervention began in the month of March, the reconstitution seemed to have a visible impact on the staff of the building. The looming deadline created additional stress and pressure for the building's teachers and related services staff. In addition, the school had a very large proportion of new teachers and a high staff turnover rate, which contributed to a pervasive feeling of instability and a constantly changing climate within the building. Although not uncommon for the district, the building had a principal who was in her first year at this elementary school. However, she was the first principal in 10 years who did not receive placement at the school as a last stop before retirement.

The Role of the Principal

Although bright and very passionate about her position, the school's first-year principal was often required to work outside the building due to additional administrative responsibilities within the large district. These supplementary duties prevented her from maintaining a consistent presence in the school and forming close relationships with many of the teachers. As a result, some teachers felt disconnected from the principal and felt that they could not depend on her regularly for guidance and support. These factors combined contributed to an often tense school climate and lack of collaborative working relationships among faculty members throughout the academic year. Even though a long-term relationship had not been cemented with the principal, there was some hope that a "young" administrator would be more dedicated to bringing about the change necessary to move the school in the right direction.

School Demographics

When considering the annual state report card scores, my placement elementary school was designated as having a high poverty population, with 95.3% of its students classified as economically disadvantaged and a high percentage of minority students. With respect to race and ethnicity, 88.5% of the students at the school are Black, non-Hispanic; 6.6% of students White, non-Hispanic; and 4.8% identified as Multiracial. In addition, 18.4% of the school's population are students with disabilities, which is notably higher than the national average of 13.1%. Despite the high number of minority students, the majority of teachers in the school are designated as White or Caucasian, which is consistent with teachers in many districts nationwide. One of these teachers became my consultee while I was at the school.

When considering the cultural context domain of the consultant–consultee relationship, the disconnect between teacher and student ethnicity and racial identity is only one facet that may comprise the problem of cultural misunderstanding. A difference in skin tone alone does not necessarily lead to poor outcomes for minority students. However, effective intrapersonal student–teacher relationships require awareness and training on the part of the teacher in order to achieve a culturally competent classroom that maintains high standards for all students.

In my consultation case, the consultee was experiencing acute pressure from many sources as well as the inability to manage the climate within his own classroom. Throughout the building, the apprehensive climate and pressure on the administration and teaching staff, combined with the external stressors of poverty, drug abuse, and mental health concerns of parents and community members, seemed to press on teachers daily. The teacher that I worked with as a consultee, Mr. K., often verbalized his perception of the stress he faced in his role as a second-grade teacher.

A former sixth-grade teacher who was new to the district, Mr. K. was a Caucasian male in his early 30s with previous teaching experience in suburban and rural districts. He was new to urban education, struggled primarily with classroom management, and often spoke of his perceived inability to relate to his students. By the time I began working with him in March, he had begun to lose his subjectivity and willingness to work with students individually. Rather, when a student was exhibiting challenging behavior, the child was punished by being sent out of the room. I believe that Mr. K. had difficulty obtaining a level of mutual respect for his students and, as a result, punished them by sending them to Positive Efforts for Adjustment and Knowledge, an in-school suspension, or by calling their parents to report bad behavior.

Though Mulvey and Cauffman (2001) cite evidence that states that "promoting healthy relationships and environments is more effective for reducing school misconduct and crime than instituting punitive penalties" (p. 800), Mr. K. believed that by "laying down the law" and by implementing authoritative punishment practices, he could demand the respect of his students. Unfortunately, this ineffective method of discipline worked to further divide the teacher from the needs of his students.

Consultant–Consultee Relationship

My relationship with the consultee began by establishing rapport through structured conversation. As a student consultant, I spoke with the client about my own educational background and my previous experiences in urban schools both as an observer and as a school psychologist in training. Through the use of the consultee-centered consultation model, I began utilizing my early interactions with the teacher to assess his areas of need. After Mr. K. gave me an extensive list of students he believed were in need of a behavioral intervention, we decided together that a classroom-wide intervention would be most suitable for his needs. However, this decision was not easily chosen, as my first suggestion of a classroom-wide intervention was not well received. In particular, the use of the "Mystery Motivator" intervention was not preferred by Mr. K., who believed that he "had already tried everything, and nothing was going to work with these kids."

Despite his feeling of disconnect with his students, I believe that Mr. K. saw me as a relatable individual, and it did not take him long to feel comfortable discussing his thoughts, opinions, and stressors with me freely and openly. Though I initially suspected that this may be due to my racial background, I now wonder if it was due to my education and former schooling in a small rural school system. Regardless of why he felt at ease with me, I believe that this relationship enabled me to initially achieve a more positive relationship with the consultee and to establish ethnic validity with the teacher. As defined by Barnett et al. (1995), ethnic validity is the "degree to which problem identification and problem solving are acceptable to the client [in this case the teacher] in respect to the client's belief and value systems, as these are associated with the client's ethnic/cultural group" (p. 221). As a first-year PhD student in a school psychology graduate program, I was in a unique consultation role where I believe the consultee did not feel intimidated or afraid to voice his concerns. Unfortunately, as our relationship continued, I found the consultee's level of comfort with me to be both a blessing and a curse, and I believe that our intervention was unsuccessful as a result.

According to a 2000 article by Collette Ingraham, it appears that "it is not the race of the consultant but the attentiveness and responsiveness of the consultant to racial issues brought up in the session that determines the ratings of consultant effectiveness and multicultural sensitivity" (p. 322). Therefore, while I believe the client felt at ease with me due to my race, I do not believe that the efficacy of the intervention was jeopardized for that reason.

Difficulty Maintaining Objectivity

As our sessions continued, Mr. K. displayed both a lack of knowledge regarding the reason he was having difficulty with behavior management in his classroom and a lack of objectivity due to characterological distortion. In addition, his attitude continued to worsen as the school year progressed, and his teaching seemed to suffer as a result. The pervasive bias of his thinking began when he became frustrated and allowed his personal anger and unhappiness with his place of work to interfere with his ability to maintain a positive relationship with his students.

As a student consultant, it became difficult for me to hear him express his frustration and anger while still maintaining the neutrality required in school consulting. Often, his comments about students would border on or surpass what I felt was inappropriate and would require me to remain silent or respond to his claim.

At times, he appeared to be filtering his perceptions of students through stereotypes and was therefore struggling with the second domain of Ingraham's (2000) multicultural school consultation framework (consultee learning and development). In those cases, I believe that his comfort level with me may have attributed to his venting of negative emotions.

In addition, theme transference due to his unsolved problems in his role as a teacher likely has impacted his inability to maintain high expectations for his classroom. These factors, as well as Mr. K.'s individual personality characteristics, may have prevented him from implementing the most effective intervention possible as a result of bias, personal expectations, and frustration with what he perceived to be his students' "inability to learn."

I believe that the consultee shared many personal stories and complaints with me as a consultant after I established rapport and presented myself as a trustworthy and understanding figure. As time passed, I was able to obtain a certain amount of expert power with the client as I shared my knowledge of behavioral interventions and discussed which ones to implement in his classroom. However, I still felt limited in what I could accomplish with the teacher due to his lack of focus on his students and negative attitude about what his classroom was able to accomplish. Additionally, his inability and unwillingness to connect with his students was very apparent, and he did little to learn their interests or preferred activities as the school year went on.

Communication Skills

In our first few sessions, the consultee approached our consultation sessions hesitantly, saying that he did not believe that his students would be receptive to any sort of rewards system. He discussed his frustration with this particular group of students and his belief that they were incapable of understanding a rewards system and being motivated by its rewards. Although I offered to provide simple directions and a way to post the intervention in the classroom, he was resistant to the idea of incorporating anything new into his classroom. He seemed to believe that his students had a different set of values and therefore would not benefit from what he had to offer. This defeated attitude became increasingly obvious as our sessions progressed.

When I videotaped one of my first consulting sessions with the teacher, he was unable to sit still or remain seated as he talked to me. He angrily paced around the room and in conversations often resorted to complaints about the students, the school, and the parents of the children in his classroom. He was also unable to "recognize that constructive relationships with parents facilitate the learning process for students" (Goldstein & Brooks, 2007, p. 192). He frequently placed calls to parents when children misbehaved but could not comprehend why parents viewed him negatively and became increasingly withdrawn from their child's education.

As I continued working with this consultee, he continued to open up to me, which led to my own realization that although empathy and the ability to "get inside the client's world" (Kampwirth & Powers, 2012, p. 123) are crucial to developing a collaborative relationship with the consultee, they may also lead to decreased productivity and negativity during consultation sessions. It was often difficult to redirect the teacher back to helping the students and even more of a struggle to refocus on the subject of the intervention.

Before beginning to take data, I became a bit worried about treatment integrity and the teacher consistently taking data, especially considering his self-reported stress level. Research has shown that the inability of a teacher to relate to his students culturally limits his ability to form positive relationships and mutual trust with those children. His negative comments reflected the lower standards he had for this "abnormal" (his words) group of students who he believed were incapable of learning a rewards system consistent with that of the intervention we chose to implement: the Mystery Motivator intervention.

As a consultant, it was evident to me that there were many factors influencing my difficulty in communicating in an effective manner with the consultee. Many stressors impacted Mr. K.'s daily life, including the possible need to find a new job in the coming months, behavior and academic problems in his class, pressure from administrators and the district to increase his class's test scores, and the need for an additional reading endorsement due to the upcoming state's Third Grade Reading Guarantee. With so many external forces impinging on our consultant–consultee relationship, it was very difficult for the teacher to focus on the intervention, and I believe that it was less effective as a result.

As discussed by Ingraham (2000), a person's personal issues can make it difficult for him or her to embrace cross-cultural situations in a constructive manner. Furthermore, there are certain unproductive outcomes that often stem from the interaction of personal needs and cross-cultural situations, and one of these applies to this case. I believe that reactive dominance was also an issue in this case. Reactive dominance occurs when "the consultee reacts to the collision of his own needs with the complexities of cross-cultural interaction by asserting dominance or imposing their patterns of thinking on the interaction" (p. 333). While working with Mr. K., it became clear to me as a consultant that his needs had gotten in the way of his taking ownership of the problems in his class. His focus had shifted to his intrapersonal needs and therefore had taken away his ability to maintain healthy interactions with his students.

Problem-Solving Process

The multicultural school consultation framework developed by Ingraham in 2000 was utilized as a foundation for the problem-solving process in this consultation case. Defined as "a culturally sensitive, indirect service in which the consultant adjusts the consultation services to address the needs and cultural value of the consultee or the client" (Ingraham, 2000, p. 325), this framework allowed me to consider the many facets of diversity and cultural interaction during my time with the consultee.

Problem Identification

As I began the consultation problem-solving process with the consultee, I found that it was very difficult to move through the steps in a timely manner. The teacher wanted to focus on numerous problems, but many were difficult to put into measurable and observable terms. Though there were many behavioral problems occurring in the classroom, I observed the classroom with the desire to make a lasting change in an intervention that required only several weeks to implement. After sitting in the classroom as an observer on numerous occasions, I was able to see that transitions—especially those between classrooms, before and after lunch and recess, and to and from the bathrooms—took a shocking amount of time. Mr. K. would instruct his students to line up along the wall, stand inside a square, and not touch each other before leaving the classroom. The students would often stand in the same spot waiting on their classmates for over 10 min before they were permitted to leave the classroom. After considering that there were eight of these transitions per day, I felt that by reducing the time required for these transitions, we could not only reduce instances of behavioral problems but also increase academic learning time.

After taking a more direct approach as a consultant, I was able to help the consultee to choose a goal of reducing the end-of-day transition period from an average baseline time of over 13 min to the goal of under 10 min. Although I considered a variety of evidence-based classroom interventions, I chose to suggest the evidence-based Mystery Motivator intervention. The teacher finally agreed to use this intervention with his students, and we chose to implement it the following week.

Though the terminal goal was set to reduce the end-of-day transition to less than 6 min, the primary goal was to reduce the transition to less than 10 min so that it was initially attainable and would allow the students to receive the reinforcement fairly easily.

Intervention Design and Planning

The Mystery Motivator (Rhode, Jenson, & Reavis, 1992) is an intervention that can be used to work with a variety of problem behaviors in the school, such as talking out of turn, turning in assignments, or fighting. It uses a random reward schedule to reinforce good behavior. It can be implemented with an individual student or with an entire classroom.

In this case, the Mystery Motivator was designed to reward classroom-wide behavior if students were able to complete the end-of-day transition in a timely manner. They were instructed to get their coats and backpacks from the coatroom and to be quiet and in their seats in less than 10 min. An intervention script, or procedures list, was used to ensure consistency in the implementation of the intervention. Mr. K. was instructed to prompt the students and inform them that he would begin timing for the end-of-day intervention. He would remind them that their goal was 10 min and encourage them to complete the transition in under that time to receive a reward. The teacher was also encouraged to show enthusiasm and to "pump up" the students to keep them excited about the Mystery Motivator intervention. This intervention was selected because it required a relatively small time commitment and not much additional effort or resources on the part of the teacher. He was able to time the transition and record the data on a sheet that was located on the wall next to the Mystery Motivator marker sheet that was used when the children met their goal for the day. By using an intervention with a small time commitment, I was able to add a minimal amount of stress to the teacher's already-hectic schedule.

Intervention Implementation

After baseline data were taken and we prepared for implementation of the Mystery Motivator, the teacher was given an intervention script, or procedures list, to ensure consistent implementation; a data sheet to record the elapsed time between the prompt and when the students were ready; and the Mystery Motivator sheet for the students to color in if they achieved their daily goal. The consultee was given the responsibilities of following the procedures each day and recording the data and was told that the consultant would return to follow up within the week. He was also advised to contact the consultant directly if he had any questions regarding the Mystery Motivator.

Integrity was checked on the first day of implementation, and I found that the intervention script was being followed accurately. On the first day of the intervention, the time recorded was 4 min 18 s, which was less than half the goal of 10 min. This showed that the students were capable of completing the transition in much less time than the goal we set. The class was visibly excited about the Mystery Motivator chart and their chance to earn a reward for good behavior. However, on the second, third, and fourth days of the intervention, the students obtained times very close to the goal of 10 min. I was unable to witness these other dates of the implementation of the intervention, but the results indicate that students were much less motivated following the first date. I believe that a good deal of the students' enthusiasm witnessed on the first intervention date was due to the children reflecting the emotions of their teacher. By seeing Mr. K. excited about a new concept for the classroom, the students became enthusiastic as well.

Unfortunately, I do not believe that the consultee was able to sustain a high level of energy or motivation for implementing the intervention effectively.

A second integrity check was scheduled, but unfortunately the teacher canceled due to state testing. The check was rescheduled to be completed the following week and was observed to be implemented almost correctly. The teacher was observed to give abbreviated instructions and to display a lack of enthusiasm for the activity. In addition, after the students were dismissed for the day, he expressed his desire to be finished with the Mystery Motivator, as he was "counting down the days until the end of school."

Evaluation of Intervention

Much of the consultant–consultee relationship focused on analyzing forces impinging on the problems in the classroom. Notably, the teacher believed that his students were unable to learn and follow directions and that this was causing poor behavioral management. As a result, it was difficult to redirect him and keep him optimistic regarding the possible results of the intervention. His bias and lack of objectivity, as evidenced by his numerous comments and frustration, likely limited him from maintaining high expectations and treatment integrity during the intervention.

Although the first session following the intervention of the Mystery Motivator resulted in a dramatic drop in transition time, the following two sessions did not result in the class earning the opportunity to color in a square on the chart. On the third date, the class met the goal by being under by 30. In the following weeks, the class met the goal 1 out of 4 times, and during each session the consultee voiced his dismay with the results. In conclusion, the results from the intervention were inconclusive in determining that this intervention was effective. However, the lessons learned by the consultant were noteworthy when considering the impact of culture and diversity on a consultation case.

Closure

At our final meeting, after 8 weeks of intervention and the collection of baseline data, I spoke with the consultee about his experience with the implementation of the Mystery Motivator intervention. Unfortunately, he continued to voice many of the same concerns he had upon our first meeting and expressed his desire to teach in a different school building the following year. Although he thanked me for coming into the school, he also seemed reluctant to try another intervention in the future.

In the end, I found it difficult to empathize with him and had even begun to feel uncomfortable toward the conclusion of our consultant–consultee relationship. I often felt that the rapport I had established had acted as a "free pass" for Mr. K. to vent his frustration to me, and I struggled with neutrality and my defense of his students. Teachers who do not display cultural competence do both the students and themselves a disservice by limiting relationships and the overall level of understanding in the classroom. In this particular case, both cultural and personal factors influenced the efficacy of the Mystery Motivator intervention. I believe that as a result, this ultimately led to an ineffective implementation of an evidence-based intervention that has proven effective in many other cases.

Diversity Issues

While working with Mr. K., a young teacher who lived outside the district and felt unprepared to work with an urban population, issues of diversity became evident each time we met. Though several of the teachers had been at the school for many years and felt comfortable with the population, Mr. K. felt that he could not relate to his students or their parents. He went as far as to say that he would not have as many behavioral issues if he were working with "normal kids at a normal school."

This comment alerted me to the consultee's belief that he was not like his students and that the school where he worked had very different norms from those he was used to. The teacher seemed to be unaware of the effects that living in poverty had on his students and was unforgiving and unaccepting of the individual differences of these students. Mr. K. failed to consider the difference in home life responsibilities between many of his students and what he had experienced growing up. He had grown up in a middle-class household and currently resided in an upper-middle-class suburb of the city. Although I cannot say that money was never a concern for him, he was well taken care of as a child and could not understand why some parents may not be able to provide homework support and guidance during after-school hours. With many single-parent households, transient living situations, parents working multiple jobs, and a high rate of drug and alcohol abuse in the neighborhood, his students often had more responsibilities at home than most students at an elementary school level. Often, these second graders would either be watched by an older sibling or would be taking care of younger siblings during the evening, leaving them little time and resources to complete homework.

However, rather than valuing the increased independence required of many of his young students, he became angry with their lack of supervision and unwillingness to complete assignments. Completing these additional responsibilities within the home was seen as a negative trait by the teacher because they were unable to fit into his perceptions of obedience and a teacher-directed classroom. Ingraham (2000) notes that:

> It is difficult for one to understand the impact of culture on others unless one has read extensively in the area or interacted with culturally different individuals who have articulated their perceptions, such as might occur in a multicultural group experience or specialized training.
>
> (p. 328)

Although Mr. K. could not understand how there might be a lack of structure for these children at home or that it may have an impact on students' ability to take orders from teachers, he may have never received training to address effective cross-cultural communication. In the end, he struggled to view the children from an ecological perspective and could only view them from a deficit perspective.

The often tedious types of assignments that Mr. K. utilized in the classroom were very difficult for students of the second-grade level and required sustained and focused attention on largely uninteresting material such as packets of multiple worksheets and written math problems. I could see that he chose to resort to these types of assignments when he was not well prepared for the lesson or had other stressors on his mind. Without guidance and effective and active teaching, students at such a young age often find it difficult to harness the intrinsic motivation to complete tedious assignments and attend to classroom activities. Therefore, I reasoned that a Mystery Motivator intervention would provide the extrinsic motivation needed to scaffold the class up to a more productive performance level.

Goldstein and Brooks (2007) list in their criteria for the *Mindset of Effective Educators* that we need to "recognize that if educators are to relate effectively to students, they must be empathic, always attempting to perceive the world through the eyes of the student" (p. 191). I believe that it is very difficult for a teacher such as Mr. K. to see the world through the eyes of the student if he or she is not aware of cultural differences and the impact that a child's socioeconomic status, language differences, and home environment can have on his or her behavior in the classroom. In this case, even the amount of total academic learning time suffered in the classroom due to the consultee's inability to relate effectively to his students. With a lack of mutual understanding and respect, his students would often disobey orders or not listen to Mr. K.'s directions. As a result, transitions in the classroom took much longer than they should have and significantly reduced active learning time for the students.

Lessons Learned

My opportunity to work as a graduate student school consultant allowed me to learn a great deal about consultant–consultee relationships and the impact of diversity on human interaction. I believe that although my role as a student made me more relatable and helped me to gain referent power, this power ultimately led me down a bit of a "slippery slope" as a consultant. After the consultee became more comfortable with me, he often voiced his negative opinions about many issues and even overshared a good deal of personal and school information during our sessions.

Ingraham (2000) defines cultural saliency as how the members of the consultation process perceive each other. This includes the assumption that both the consultant and the consultee operate from their own cultural identities, experiences, and contexts. Thus, cultural saliency focuses on the elements of one's identity that are raised in another's awareness during the cross-cultural interaction. I believe that I began to experience difficulty when I adjusted my own frame of reference to match the consultee's reference point. By adjusting my lens to maintain rapport with the client and attempting to bridge this cultural gap, I may have inadvertently blurred my own lines of cultural competence.

According to Ingraham (2000), "consultants working within multicultural settings need knowledge, skills, and attitudes to (a) attend simultaneously to the perspectives of their consultee, client, and themselves; and (b) create bridges of understanding that link the distinct perspectives of each" (p. 326). In this case, I worked with a teacher who was culturally very different from many of his students. Mr. K. was often unable to bridge this cultural gap in order to facilitate positive teacher–student relationships. This experience helped me to realize the importance of cultural competence and the adequate training of teachers in order to prepare them for working in urban school districts. Mr. K. told me during a consultation session that he "thought [he] was good at classroom management until he came [to this school]." Although the United States has an increasingly diverse population, the majority of classroom teachers continue to identify as White or Caucasian. In addition, many teachers who lack experience in working with urban populations may find it difficult to manage classroom behavior, and therefore these teachers have a high turnover rate. Mr. K. told me at the conclusion of our sessions that he would not be reapplying for his job next year; rather, he would be looking for a job in the suburbs.

I believe that while this case allowed me to find my passion in helping to train professionals in cultural competence, I felt limited in my ability to immediately help remediate the problems in the classroom. Although I was able to build relationships with many of his students during my time in the classroom, it pained me to see the strained relationships and negativity in Mr. K.'s class. Being a novice consultant, I found it difficult not to overstep my boundaries as a consultant in training but also to not remain silent and to not attempt to better the situation. Without adequate training for classroom teachers in multicultural competence, research has shown that this divide may continue to exist for many individuals. Had I been a practitioner in the school, I may have been able to implement professional development training on the topic or better advocate for related training from an outside consultant.

In conclusion, much of my experience in implementing the Mystery Motivator intervention revolved around getting past the personal issues of the teacher and the diversity-related conflicts and keeping the sessions focused on what was best for the children. This made it very difficult to help the consultee improve his classroom transitions and implement an effective intervention. I believe that in the future I will use my experience with Mr. K. to help me guide sessions through a more direct approach and work harder to keep the focus on the students rather than on the teacher's own personal struggles and difficulties. In addition, I will take what I have learned through the supervision process to continue to grow in the area of culturally competent consultation. Overall, although it was difficult at times, I appreciated this opportunity to learn and grow as a future consultant in the schools.

Questions for Reflection

- What could have been done to avoid the "slippery slope" experienced by the consultant in this case?
- What is the role of the consultant in encouraging culturally relevant pedagogy and the cultural understanding of his or her consultee?
- If a consultee shows reluctance to continue with an intervention, what should be done to address whether to continue or discontinue implementation?

References

Barnett, D. W., Collins, R., Coulter, C., Curtis, M. J., Ehrhardt, K., Glaser, A. . . . Winston, M. (1995). Ethnic validity and school psychology: Concepts and practices associated with cross-cultural professional competence. *Journal of School Psychology, 33*, 219–234.

Bronfenbrenner, U. (1989). Ecological systems theory. *Annals of Child Development, 6*, 982–1022.

Goldstein, S., & Brooks, R. B. (2007). *Understanding and managing children's classroom behavior: creating sustainable, resilient classrooms.* Hoboken, NJ: Wiley & Sons.

Ingraham, C. L. (2000). Consultation through a multicultural lens: Multicultural and cross-cultural consultation in schools. *School Psychology Review, 29*, 320–343.

Kampwirth, T. J., & Powers, K. M. (2012). *Collaborative consultation in the schools: Effective practices for students with learning and behavior problems.* Upper Saddle River, NJ: Pearson.

Mulvey, E., & Cauffman, E. (2001). The inherent limits of predicting school violence. *American Psychologist, 56*, 797–802.

Rhode, G., Jenson, W. R., & Reavis, H. K. (1992). *The tough kid book.* Longmont, CO: Sopris West.

Rosenfield, S. (2012). Becoming a school consultant: Lessons learned. New York, NY: Routledge.

4

WORKING AGAINST THE SCHOOL-TO-PRISON PIPELINE

Lessons From a Novice Consultant

Amy Bremer

Advance Organizer Questions

- What skills will the consultant need to utilize to provide effective consultation when the consultee is closed off from collaborative problem solving?
- What role do problem-solving teams have in the consultation relationship in overcoming barriers to effective interventions?
- What are some components of this case that must be addressed prior to the implementation of a successful intervention?

School Ecology

The following case occurred during my school psychology internship. Although I had experience in school-based consultation through practicum experiences, my consultation skills were still developing, particularly with respect to navigating barriers. Naturally, school-based factors are likely to have an impact on the consulting relationship and thus should be considered by the consultant. In the case presented below, a variety of school-based factors are presented for consideration in analyzing the consulting relationship. Train Elementary is a school located in a large urban district. During the time this case occurred, the school was undergoing significant changes, which included new administration and staff. In the previous year, the school was reconstituted, replacing all but two teachers due to poor performance on standardized tests and state report cards. This school year, the school was assigned a new principal and leadership intern (principal in training). Train Elementary is connected to a separate school designated for students with emotional and behavioral disorders. Though separate schools, they share common areas and some support staff.

Train Elementary has a reputation in the district for having "behavior problems" and is located in a predominantly African American neighborhood with a high prevalence of violence, crime, and poverty. Housing in the area is primarily government subsidized. Safety in the neighborhood is a concern of many parents. Through informal conversations with parents, I learned that many do not let their children play outside for fear for their safety.

Role of Administration

The impact of the administrative changes in the school was extremely salient to me. The newly assigned principal, Mr. Ellis, is an African American male who greeted everyone with a hug. He is an experienced principal who had made progress in his previous schools (per school report cards). Staff perception was that administration changes were for the better. Mr. Ellis gave the impression of a stern but caring and warm authoritative figure, and one school staff member shared with me that she felt that the school really needed an African American male principal like him. The leadership intern assigned to the building, Mrs. Carl, was also African American and grew up in the surrounding neighborhood. She was engaging and knowledgeable on evidence-based practices as well as passionate and committed to the school. She was well liked and easily captured the respect of teachers, parents, and students. As one teacher described it, when her class heard Mrs. Carl's heels coming down the hall, they all made sure that they were on their best behavior. The administration worked well as a team, making many positive changes in the school, including implementing schoolwide positive behavior support strategies.

School Climate

A school's climate has a major impact on its capacity to develop engaged learners and promote academic and life success. The climate of Train Elementary was stressed but seemed to be moving in a positive direction. The majority of the staff bought into the changes being made by the administration, but feelings of frustration and stress associated with the many internal and external challenges facing this school were palpable. The relationships between most school staff and the administration were generally positive; however, being a newly formed staff, camaraderie and relationships between staff members were still in development. Staff tension existed, with staff members perceived as getting in the way of progress. The many emotional and behavioral needs of the students, barriers to learning associated with poverty, and the culture of violence in the neighborhood placed strain on the staff and students. I observed (and experienced!) frustration related to feelings of ineffectiveness or inability to make change, as well as pressure to produce change in spite of ongoing unmet needs.

Parent–school connection was also poor. Initiatives put into place to involve and engage parents appeared to have some impact, such as parent nights and efforts to increase positive communication with parents. Several parents shared with me that they felt that the school was more receptive to parents than in previous years. However, reaching parents was difficult, and for many parents, involvement in the school was limited to school discipline hearings.

Some of the positive changes in school climate were attributed to moderate improvements in schoolwide behavior. The schoolwide positive behavior program appeared to be successful in developing expectations of behaviors, consistency in routines, and holding teachers accountable for follow-through. Behaviors were improved from the previous year with the office and hallways appearing much calmer.

School Discipline and Behavior Management

When consultation is focused on students with disruptive behaviors, a school's ability to manage behavior effectively and the disciplinary procedures in place are likely to impact the effectiveness of interventions. In line with evidence-based practices in implementing schoolwide positive behavior supports, assemblies were held at the beginning of the school year to teach all students the expected school behavior, which was also reinforced by classroom lessons. Posters supporting this program were hung around the school, and teachers were expected to use common language. A schoolwide reinforcement contingency was put in place, and time was designated each day for teachers to document the behavior of each student in their class. This appeared to be effective in developing consistent expectations but did not address teacher and staff capacity to use positive behavior management strategies in the classroom. There was a tendency toward yelling and use of coercive language when dealing with noncompliance and challenging behaviors that persisted, particularly for those teachers with limited skills in positive behavior management. To my knowledge, no formal staff training in positive behavior management was conducted. Underscoring the need for all staff members to be trained in these strategies, office staff, who played an integral role in the school discipline process, had particularly negative styles of communicating with students. Despite positive behavior strategies, exclusionary practices and punishment remained the "go-to" methods for managing behavior.

Multicultural School Consultation

In the framework of multicultural school consultation (MSC), Ingraham (2000, 2003) outlines competencies of culturally competent consultants as well as the cultural factors that may influence the consultation process. Thus, the consultant must consider the cultural influences of the consultant, consultee, and client, as well as the cultural context in which the consultation occurs. Prior coursework in diversity and cultural influences on education, as well as previous practicum experiences, provided opportunities for me to reflect on my own cultural biases and worldview and gain insight and knowledge into the implications of diversity on the consultation process. Through my practicum experiences, I had improved my communication skills and developed a foundational understanding of the problem-solving process. I still considered myself a novice consultant because in order to move beyond my current level, I needed more practice in combining my emerging knowledge and awareness of cultural and diversity influences with consultation skills in real-world experiences. In particular, practice and experience are needed to develop skills in navigating a range of barriers to effective consultation within an MSC framework.

Problem-Solving Teams

The context of a multidisciplinary problem-solving team is important for understanding the consultation relationship and the case as a whole, as the building team plays a central role in initiating consultation. In this instance, the role of the consultant applies to both the problem-solving team as well as myself. The problem-solving team was in the early stages of implementing a case manager model of consultation. According to the model, when cases were referred to the team, they were assigned a case manager. Following a referral, the problem-solving team meets to determine appropriate interventions for the presenting problem. The case manager or direct consultant is then responsible for guiding data-based decision making and working with the teacher in implementing team recommendations. This process had been piloted the year before and was now being fully implemented for the first year.

The problem-solving team consisted of White, African American, and Latina teachers and support staff (all female) with varying levels of professional experience. Mrs. Night was an African American female in her mid-40s. I am a White female in my late 20s. Generally speaking, communication styles between team members was direct and forward, but I did observe some differences between team members of different races. White team members appeared to be more apologetic and less comfortable with the direct communication style. I viewed this style of communication as an interchange between the influence of the overall culture of the school and the individual cultural influences of the team members. As my involvement with the team and my consultation with Mrs. Night continued, my ability to match this style of communication progressed. I think that a lack of comfort with communicating in a direct manner posed some limitations for me early on—more so in the context of one-on-one consultation with Mrs. Night. In the context of the problem-solving team, the school psychologist was viewed as the decision maker in many ways, so in the context of the team, I had more social capital, which aided in my comfort level in matching the communication style of the team. In one-on-one consultation, I believe that Mrs. Night viewed herself as the expert, which I believe impacted my ability to adjust to cultural differences in communication styles.

Teacher Characteristics

Mrs. Night was a first-year teacher who had previously worked as a counselor in behavioral health and trauma care. At the initial team meeting, she did not appear willing to collaborate with others on interventions and made known her experience in developing behavior plans. Her interactions with others were primarily one sided. I observed her taking control of conversations and ending the conversation before hearing from the other person. This was typical of my interactions with her as well. During most of our conversations, it seemed as if she had one foot out the door, and she was not agreeable to scheduling formal times to meet. I found this challenging because I could not arrange set times to meet with her and had to seek her out frequently in order to catch her at a free moment, making planning a challenge.

Factors related to a consultee's openness toward consultation and awareness of one's own skill level need to be considered by the consultant. Personal issues, such as need for control, may make it difficult to approach cultural issues in a constructive manner. A consultee who has a need for control may assert a particular course of action or belief, regardless of its appropriateness for the client; this is known as reactive dominance (Ingraham, 2000, 2003). My observations of Mrs. Night's teaching style indicated that she possessed limited classroom management skills. Her interactions with students were negatively toned, and if the classroom became chaotic, she would appear stressed and tended toward yelling. Throughout the consultation relationship, she frequently focused on a student's history of trauma as the primary problem, suggesting that she needed to understand what traumas he had experienced. However, she provided no information to support trauma as the prominent issue for him. In this case, it seemed that Mrs. Night clung tightly to her worldview of how best to intervene for this student based on her past experience in trauma care rather than the presenting issues of the client or an examination of other factors in the child's environment that might contribute to the problem. She also frequently referenced her experience in behavior management; however, she did not seem to be aware of how being a novice teacher impacted her ability to implement effective classroom management. My perspective on this is that she wanted to present herself as an expert and therefore was less open to consultation in order to control the narrative and protect that persona.

Collaborative Relationship

The student in this consultation case was referred through the problem-solving team, and therefore the consultant–consultee relationship was established through this process. Following the initial problem-solving team meeting, I shared with Mrs. Night that I would be counseling Mark to develop anger management skills. She had left the meeting early and therefore was not aware of all the team's recommendations. This was a problematic start to our collaboration, but one that I had no control over. She expressed that she did not care for the plan because work completion was her primary concern. I explained that this would be in addition to classroom-based behavior intervention that she would be putting in place and that our efforts could work in tandem with one another, hoping to establish an avenue for collaboration. By the end of our initial conversation, she appeared more open toward my involvement. Aware that Mrs. Night did not enter this consulting relationship willingly but that this was expected as a result of her coming to the problem-solving team, during our next several encounters I attempted to establish rapport by employing attentive listening and empathy skills. However, I was unsuccessful in turning the conversation toward collaborative problem solving, and our communication remained primarily one sided.

The Problem-Solving Process

Mark was referred to the problem-solving team by his mother because of concerns regarding frequent behavior referrals and academic underachievement. Mark is African American and was in fifth grade at the time of the referral. The initial interview was conducted during a problem-solving team meeting. This format may be a common experience of school psychologists or school-based consultants who are involved with school problem-solving teams or intervention assistance teams. Such a structure may pose additional challenges as well as benefits in managing the dynamics of a team of individuals in establishing effective multicultural consultation that is typically not the focus of consultation research.

Both Mark's mother and teacher attended the meeting, although neither was present for the duration of the meeting. His mother arrived late, and Mrs. Night left the meeting early. Mrs. Night reported that Mark displayed disruptive behavior in the classroom. She described him as intelligent and believed that he was underperforming in the classroom. She also described him as a class clown. Specifically, she reported that he often appeared in a daze or tired, used inappropriate language, bothered peers purposefully, completed very little classroom work, and became argumentative when getting into trouble. His teacher also shared that she was concerned that his allergies were affecting him in school. Her primary concern was completion of classroom work. While Mrs. Night appeared to be genuinely concerned about Mark, she also appeared to be blaming the parent who was not present at this time by noting a lack of communication and ability to manage Mark's allergies. Throughout the intervention period, I interacted frequently with Mark's mother to communicate skills targeted and progress. His mother expressed limited communication from Mark's teacher. Communication between home and school seemed to be limited, despite perceived willingness from the parent. I believe that Mrs. Night expected Mark's mother to initiate communication with her rather than making more concerted efforts to increase collaborative home–school communication.

At the initial meeting, his mother reported that Mark lived at home with his mother and younger sister, was diagnosed with ADHD, and suffered from allergies. Mark's mother shared that in fourth grade he was referred for the gifted and talented program, but she "never followed up on it." His mother described him as a very capable and smart young man but said that she had trouble getting him to do his work and that he often did not bring his homework home. She similarly reported that he becomes defiant and argumentative and often lies when he gets into trouble.

Mark has a history of behavioral referrals related to classroom disruption. A review of benchmark assessments showed at- or above-grade-level academic skills areas. The problem-solving team recommended behavior interventions to target classroom work and remaining on task. Despite the case manager and consultation model being implemented, Mrs. Night decided that she would serve as her own case manager and left the meeting early. Anticipating challenges with teacher follow-through and intervention integrity, the problem-solving team recommended that I conduct counseling with Mark to develop anger management skills as an additional component to the intervention. A referral to the school nurse was also made to discuss management of allergies with the parent.

I observed Mark for a few minutes each week prior to counseling sessions. I also observed his interactions with office staff on several occasions because my office was located in the main office. Consistent with the teacher's reports, he was often not paying attention and was at times sleeping in class. His classroom was often dark and was not very engaging. On several occasions, Mrs. Night complained to me about Mark's behavior in front of him and the rest of his class. I also observed several arguments between him and Mrs. Night. Mark would become reactive and argumentative and deny involvement when Mrs. Night accused him of doing something. These arguments escalated quickly and often resulted in a more serious consequence for Mark. When given an opportunity to cool off and discuss the issue at hand, he was more willing to accept a consequence and acknowledge and take responsibility for his actions, and the conflict subsequently subsided. However, this sequence of events was uncommon. When he was referred to the office, conflict continued between Mark and office staff, providing four to five different negative interactions within a short period of time. In absence of conflict and emotional stress, Mark was kind, polite, and outgoing. During my counseling sessions with Mark, he was talkative, active, and high energy. He could also be very insightful and self-reflective when engaged in problem solving and appeared motivated to improve his behavior.

Defining the Problem

Mark's off-task behaviors in the classroom (not paying attention, bothering peers) and failure to complete schoolwork appeared to be maintained by avoidance of work and attention from his peers. Though capable, Mark was not engaged in learning, which was further compromised by his relationship with his teacher and other school personnel. Recent research suggests that a student's social relationship with peers, adults at school, and family members has significant influence on behavior (Harris, 2006). Exacerbating the issue of school engagement, Mark possessed limited self-management and emotional regulation skills, which resulted in frequent office referrals and, consequently, exclusion from the learning environment.

Strengths and Protective Factors

- Intelligent
- Funny and charismatic
- Insightful
- Self-reflection skills
- Strong parent support
- Likes to read for fun
- Positive relationships with one or more school staff members

Weaknesses and Risk Factors

- Social–emotional skills (anger management and conflict resolution, self-management, impulse control)
- Disengaged from learning
- Relationship with teacher and some school staff
- Frequent suspensions
- Classroom climate
- Poor learning environment
- Home–school relationship
- African American
- Exposure to violence and crime
- Health (allergies)

Intervention Implementation

As recommended by the problem-solving team, Mrs. Night was to conduct a classroom behavior intervention targeting work completion. Points were earned for class participation, following directions, and completing work and were banked using an online tracking program. Points could be used for items in the teacher's prize box. Classroom-based behavior intervention was not developed collaboratively. At the same time, I conducted counseling with Mark, targeting self-management skills. Sessions occurred weekly for about three months, though consistency was a barrier due to suspensions that occurred during this time period. Modeling and repeated practice were used as an evidence-based behavioral procedure for developing appropriate skills. We created a "drill" together that included steps to stop, think, and listen. Skills were reviewed during each session. Information and ways to promote these skills were provided to both Mrs. Night and his mother in order to promote the use of learned skills at home and in the classroom.

Evaluation

The intervention period was approximately three months. During this time, Mark was referred to the office six times for behavior, resulting in a total of 14 days of out-of-school suspension. This interfered with consistency and limited the effectiveness of the interventions. In the context of counseling, Mark made progress on learning and recalling steps for targeted skills, and as sessions progressed he gained more independence in executing the drill in practice situations. I had also observed him using the drill with other school personnel, suggesting some generalization of the skills. It is unclear how much targeted skills generalized to the classroom setting due to the lack of data produced, but no impact was seen on the rate of suspensions. Similarly, evaluation of classroom-based interventions is difficult due to the lack of data provided. A follow-up team meeting was held to review progress of the interventions. I specifically requested this meeting due to the inability to develop a collaborative relationship with Mrs. Night and concern regarding intervention effectiveness. By this time, I had developed more comfort and confidence in leading problem-solving team meetings with a more direct communication style. Mrs. Night arrived late to the meeting without intervention data. She explained her intervention, which was essentially the classroom-wide program and was not individualized to meet Mark's needs. She stated that she could not do rewards "just for him" and provided an intervention plan that was vague. The intervention plan did not include measurable goals, and the reinforcement offered (a classroom treasure box) was not reinforcing to Mark. In counseling, Mark had specifically stated that he did not care for anything in the treasure box, but identified several items that would be reinforcing to him, some as simple as coloring sheets. Student buy-in was not a concern in counseling but likely had an impact on classroom-based strategies. Mrs. Night appeared to be offended that the intervention plan needed to be adjusted. Yet, interestingly, in subsequent interactions she was more open to collaboration. Following the second formal problem-solving meeting, some initial steps were made toward a more collaborative relationship; however, Mark withdrew from the school and enrolled in an online school before any modifications to the intervention could be implemented.

Closure

From the beginning of the consultation relationship, issues emerged regarding the roles and expectations of the consultee, which impacted the effectiveness of the intervention. Mrs. Night was often evasive and dominated conversations, posing significant challenges for me in developing a collaborative relationship with her. This pattern of interaction was not limited to consultation between the two of us but manifested itself in team meetings and interaction with other team members. The absence of a voluntary, collaborative relationship directly impeded the intervention implementation. This caused a significant amount of frustration for me; however, I did notice some change in the relationship toward collaboration as I began to mirror her direct style of communication.

Diversity Issues

Exploration of the role of diversity and culture in school consultation is driven by awareness and understanding of the impact that cultural issues may have on the effectiveness of the consultation process, as well as the need for a culturally competent framework for practice. Contextual and power influences are among the cultural influences outlined by the MSC framework that need to be considered in order to engage in effective multicultural consultation. Consultants are charged with the task of evaluating and determining the extent to which such contextual and societal influences may be impacting the presenting problem. Analysis of the risk factors and barriers to learning that Mark was experiencing reveals that several issues of diversity are apparent that must be considered in order to address his needs effectively. The school-to-prison pipeline (STPP) was a particularly salient sociocultural factor in this case, providing both cultural and power influences. The STPP, which disproportionately affects students of color, refers to a cycle of negative interactions among children, their families, school personnel, and service providers that lead to or exacerbate academic and behavioral issues (McNeely & Falci, 2004). This cycle of negative interactions contributes to delinquency, arrest, and incarceration, effectively funneling students out of school and into prison systems (Osher, Woodruff, & Sims, 2002). Risk factors include poverty and race, poor social–emotional capacity, family–school disconnection, and poor school climate or conditions for learning (Osher et al., 2012). Schools have a significant impact on progression along the STPP through school disciplinary practices. Exclusionary practices (e.g., suspension and expulsion) have become standard tools for schools to manage student behavior. Though common in practice, research shows that the use of such methods is ineffective and predicts poor outcomes for youth (Wilson, 2014).

In his book *Teaching with Poverty in Mind*, Eric Jenson (2009) outlines barriers to academic and social success that children in poverty face; namely, limited social and emotional skills, acute and chronic stressors, cognitive lags, and health and safety issues. Jenson explains that the urban poor face a complex aggregate of chronic and acute stressors (including crowding, violence, and noise). Some teachers may interpret a student's social or emotional deficits as a lack of manners; however, children from poor neighborhoods are more likely to come to school with a fewer range of appropriate skills than might be expected. Students raised in poverty are more likely to display disruptive behaviors, impulsivity, and inappropriate emotional responses. Developing these skills should be done through evidence-based strategies that encourage positive relationships with adults and peers and by teaching social skills. While knowing this research, it is critically important to ascertain if this truly speaks to the issues Mark is having, always cognizant of making sure not to stereotype Mark simply because he is Black. The most disruptive and salient issues for Mark were lagging skills in the areas of self-management and accepting consequences. While he had a history of this type of behavior, I also recognized that poor classroom management over the years may have also contributed to his lagging skills in this area. When considered in the context of culture, Mark faced several risk factors (e.g., lagging skills, unmet medical needs, and chronic stress) related to poverty that interfered with his learning and engagement in school. Furthering this issue, Mark's race, frequent behavior referrals and school discipline practices, and student–teacher relationship placed Mark at significantly higher risk for progression along the STPP. In order to appropriately intervene, interventions targeting the presenting risk factors are imperative.

Lessons Learned

This case occurred during my school psychology internship, a point in time when although I had some experience in school-based consultation, my consultation skills were still developing, particularly with respect to navigating barriers. Contrary to my previous practicum experiences, on internship I was a "full-fledged" member of the school and thus my experiences more closely aligned with those of a full-time school psychologist. This experience provided me with an opportunity to continue the development of my skills, particularly in utilizing the MSC framework since I interned in a large urban school district. Mark's teacher's lack of willingness to engage in consultation impeded the effectiveness of the intervention. This did not appear to be due to a lack of knowledge of the purpose of behavior interventions or a lack of buy-in that interventions can be effective but rather seemed to be due to a desire to control the narrative and the teacher's limited awareness of her own skill level in implementing such interventions. In my previous consultation experiences on practicum, I had experienced barriers related to a teacher's ability to implement interventions and had begun to develop skills in coaching teachers in order to promote these skills. I had found that openness, flexibility, and demonstrating that I valued the teacher's input were helpful tools in engaging the consultee in the process. I believe that Mrs. Night did not view me as an equal or as someone who could provide her with assistance. Rather, she regarded her own skills as superior. Because she dominated conversations early on, I was challenged in demonstrating my skill set and in establishing referent power. It was not until I mirrored her style of communication by taking more control over conversations and utilizing the dynamics of the problem-solving team that I was able to establish myself as knowledgeable to her. I learned that in order to engage a consultee who does not view you as knowledgeable, establishing referent power is a critical step toward collaboration. Further, garnering control and demonstrating confidence may be key skills in doing so. In addition to developing my own skills as a consultant, the context of a problem-solving team may be an effective strategy for addressing teacher barriers. In this case, using the problem-solving team provided an avenue of accountability in requiring Mrs. Night to present documentation of the intervention.

In addition to teacher-related barriers, diversity issues played a significant role in the presenting problem. The capacity of the school as a whole to respond to and mediate risk factors associated with poverty and the STPP exacerbated the challenges Mark was facing. Schools play a key role in intervening in or expediting progression along the STPP. Mark's case particularly highlights how schools contribute to school disengagement and the challenges and barriers to consultation due to these factors. Teachers and school staff with poor classroom management skills turn to exclusionary tactics to essentially eliminate the problems and only teach those who "want to learn" or those who will conform (Osher et al., 2012).

School-based police officers, mandated reporting of behavioral incidents, and the use of school exclusion all contribute to a harsh disciplinary culture in schools, and zero-tolerance policies preclude educators from focusing on the individual needs of the students (Osher et al., 2012). Research supports many alternative methods for handling defiance aside from expulsion and suspensions, including positive behavioral strategies. Exclusion damages relationships between students, families, and staff, whereas establishing relationships of mutual trust, building a caring learning environment, and using positive behavioral strategies can effectively prevent and intervene in problem behavior (Coggshall, Osher, & Colombi, 2013). However, schools may be entrenched in certain policies and procedures, and even attempts at implementing evidence-based practices may be limited by the cultural competence of staff (Osher et al., 2012). Staff and schools often fail to see the bigger picture of how their procedures and behaviors contribute to the detrimental outcomes of some students with behavioral issues.

School-based consultants serving schools with high populations of students at risk for the STPP should be aware of and well versed in interventions aimed at reducing risk factors and promoting resiliency for these students. Furthermore, it is important that this be addressed from a systems perspective. Cultural competency of school psychology practice includes sensitivity to cultural issues as well as educating others about how these factors affect learning (Rogers, 1998). As a novice consultant, I experienced frustration regarding the ineffective school discipline practices and the impact these had on Mark and other students in the school. Being fully aware that frequent suspensions placed Mark at even higher risk for the STPP, I was frustrated with not knowing how best to intervene at the school level. Upon reflection, it seemed that the school personnel at Train Elementary were aware that poverty and race pose significant barriers to learning yet lacked knowledge in how schools contribute to or exacerbate these issues, particularly when considering the need to systematically teach lagging social–emotional skills. Awareness of and education on the interaction between the cultural context of poverty and school factors, as well as knowledge of evidence-based strategies, could be provided through an in-service training.

Armed with knowledge in evidence-based practices, school-based consultants are in a unique position to work with school personnel, students, and families in implementing culturally competent practices in mediating risk factors. However, garnering effective change through collective work may be hindered by any number of barriers, including sociocultural factors, staff buy-in, administration support, and staff training. Conceptualizing Mark's case within the MSC framework as well as from an ecological perspective is key in understanding the complex interactions that contribute to presenting barriers. Though I faced much frustration with this case, my experiences in this case helped me to develop skills in understanding and addressing these factors in future consultation.

Questions for Reflection

- How can problem-solving teams establish clear consultee and consultant expectations?
- What steps can be made to reverse the culture of harsh disciplinary practices and increase education on effective methods for behavior change?
- What should be included in pre-service education or in-services that can be used by consultants in order to develop an increased awareness of the role of schools in the STPP and the ways that schools can intervene?

References

Coggshall, J., Osher, D., & Colombi, G. (2013). Enhancing educators' capacity to stop the school-to-prison pipeline. *Family Court Review, 51*, 435–444.

Harris, J.R. (2006). *No two alike.* New York, NY: Norton.

Ingraham, C. (2000). Consultation through a multicultural lens: Multicultural and cross-cultural consultation in schools. *School Psychology Review, 29*, 320–343.

Ingraham, C. (2003). Multicultural consultee-centered consultation: When novice consultants explore cultural hypotheses with experienced teacher consultees. *Journal of Educational and Psychological Consultation, 14*, 329–362.

Jenson, E. (2009). *Teaching with poverty in mind: What being poor does to kids' brains and what schools can do about it.* Alexandria, VA: Association for Supervision and Curriculum Development.

McNeely, C.A., & Falci, C. (2004). School connectedness and the transition into and out of health risk behavior among adolescents: A comparison of social belonging and teacher support. *Journal of School Health, 74,* 284–292.

Osher, D., Coggshall, J., Colombi, G., Woodruff, D., Francois, S., and Osher, T. (2012). Building school and teacher capacity to eliminate the school-to-prison pipeline. *Teacher Education and Special Education, 35,* 284–295.

Osher, D., Woodruff, D., & Sims, A. (2002). Schools make a difference: The relationship between education services for African American children and youth and their over-representation in the juvenile justice system. In D. Losen (Ed.), *Minority issues in special education* (pp. 93–116). Cambridge, MA: Harvard Education Publishing Group.

Rogers, M.R. (1998). The influence of race and consultant verbal behavior on perceptions of consultant competence and multicultural sensitivity. *School Psychology Quarterly, 13,* 265–280.

Wilson, H. (2014). Turning off the school-to-prison pipeline. *Reclaiming Children and Youth, 23,* 49–53.

5

CONCEPTUALIZING PROBLEMS BY FOCUSING ON CULTURAL CONTEXT, BIAS, AND GENERALIZATION

Maggie Beard

Advance Organizer Questions

- What communication skills could help the consultee mitigate bias, solve problems, and build collaborative relationships?
- How does the consultant work with the consultee using alternate perspective taking and rewording to more accurately conceptualize the problem while at the same time allowing the consultee to change his or her perspective?

School Culture

TopCity School is an elementary school that serves children from kindergarten through fifth grade in an urban neighborhood that is considered low income. The school's population is 88.5% Black, non-Hispanic; 4.8% Multiracial; and 6.6% White, non-Hispanic. TopCity has a high-poverty building status, with 95.3% of the school population meeting the criteria for being economically disadvantaged. Around 18.4% of the school population is identified as students with disabilities. There are about 383 students on average that attend the school. My consultee described the culture of the school as one that has no parental support. She also indicated that there are a lot of differences between this school and other urban schools in the area, largely due to socio-economic status. She described the neighborhood as always changing around TopCity School. She also indicated that there are a lot of mental health issues and behavior problems for many of the kids. McCurdy, Mannella, and Eldridge (2003) explain that urban schools are seeing a large increase in antisocial behavior where there is a deep influence of poverty largely due to within-family and community-based risk factors. These findings are consistent with reports of behavior and poverty expressed by the consultee.

TopCity School has been designated as being in an academic emergency, which is the lowest designation a school can hold. TopCity has met 1 of 8 state indicators, and it has not met their annual yearly progress. The state indicators are based on state assessments and attendance and graduation rates. To earn an indicator for achievement tests, at least 75% of students must reach proficient or above for the given assessment. TopCity has failed to meet at least 75% proficiency for third- and fourth-grade math and reading achievement. It has also failed to meet at least 75% proficiency for math, reading, and science achievement in the fifth grade as well. Its performance index score is 64.6 on a scale of 0–120 points. The performance index reflects the achievement of every student enrolled for the full academic year. TopCity's value-added rating represents the progress that the school has made with its students since the last school year. In contrast, achievement scores represent students' performance at a point in time. A score of "above" indicates that greater than 1 year of progress has been achieved; "met" indicates that 1 year of progress has been achieved; and "below" indicates that less than 1 year of progress has been achieved. Since last year, TopCity has met the expected growth for the overall composite. It is above the expected growth in both reading and mathematics for Grade 4. It has met the expected growth for reading in Grade 5 and is below the expected growth for fifth-grade mathematics. Although 88.5% of the school is Black, non-Hispanic, poverty is probably the best predictor for who will struggle in school, not the student's racial minority status (Kampwirth & Powers, 2012). Under the No Child Left Behind mandates, schools are required to use scientifically validated practices in order to bring all students to a level of proficiency by the year 2017 (Rathvon, 2008). Therefore, evidence-based interventions embedded within the collaborative consultation process are gaining much attention in urban-, suburban-, and rural-area schools.

Relationship: Consultant and Consultee

According to Ingraham (2000, 2003), in the multicultural school consultation (MSC) framework, the consultant considers the influences of culture on thoughts, expectations, and behaviors from all parties within the consultation process and makes adjustments to develop and maintain rapport and understanding with the consultee. From the outset of the consultation relationship, I worked to build rapport with Ms. Stroll. I took a personal interest in her previous teaching experience, the schools that she has been at, and the things that she had to say about her abilities as a teacher. I empathized with Ms. Stroll when she told me that she had a split classroom that had been creating some problems for her. She explained that she was trying to teach first- and second-grade Common Core Standards and that she was also having a lot of behavior concerns between the two classes due to the split.

Ms. Stroll is in her 27th year of teaching, with her last 5 years spent at TopCity School. Ms. Stroll is Black, non-Hispanic, unlike the majority of the teaching staff at TopCity, who are White. There were obvious ethnic differences, but I worked to develop a positive collaborative relationship. I believe that my previous tutoring experience with low-income African American students allowed me to bridge the salient ethnic differences between myself and the consultee. I hoped to provide Ms. Stroll with support and encouragement by trying to offer intervention support for some of the behavior issues that she was experiencing with her class. Many times when she wanted just to talk about nonrelated issues, I always listened. I was often quick to compliment Ms. Stroll for certain positive things I saw her doing in the classroom that I thought would contribute to a positive intervention and relationship-building skills with her. I felt confident that I would be able to develop a positive working relationship with Ms. Stroll so that we would be able to implement and monitor the intervention.

Communication Skills

Communication skills are a vital part of the consultation process. Communication skills like paraphrasing and summarizing are important components for problem conceptualization. Effective communication skills can help coconstruct observable measurable problems by addressing a consultee's lack of objectivity. It's important to get the consultee to move past generalizations by getting them to think about other possible explanations to problems and reducing bias by rewording and refocusing the consultee on strengths rather than weaknesses of the student or students (Newman, Ingraham, & Shriberg, 2015). At our initial meeting, Ms. Stroll indicated that she would prefer that I use her personal e-mail or text her messages to her cell phone to correspond. I reached out using both methods, but many times my attempts were unsuccessful. I would have to make several attempts over a few days in order to get responses, and when she did respond via text it was one- to two-word answers. I asked her during one meeting if she could keep me updated with data points during the intervention every couple of days via e-mail. She told me that she checks e-mails but doesn't usually respond to them. Thus, the only means of true communication that we could have throughout the collaborative consultation process was to meet in person. Even then, she canceled and rescheduled often on me. Communication was difficult to arrange between the two of us. If given the opportunity to meet more, I think we would have been able to practice some of these communication skills and perhaps gain a more accurate conceptualization of the problems that were occurring.

Problem-Solving Process

Throughout the initial consultation process, it was very difficult for Ms. Stroll to really identify the one problem that she would have liked to focus the most on. Generally, she had a variety of problems. Each time, we would work to extend and better understand one of the problems and she would shift the focus to new problems or ideas. After several consultation sessions, we were finally able to come up with two problems that she was interested in targeting. One was transition time and the other was instances of bullying in the classroom. Despite my efforts to encourage her to choose only one, we finally decided to move forward with two simultaneous interventions to address both of her concerns. The bullying problem, however, is the basis of this chapter because she was not able to implement the transition time intervention accordingly or track and monitor progress.

Problem Identification: Baseline and Goal Discussion

Problem identification can be considered the most important stage during the consultation process because a positive outcome is more likely for the consultation process if this stage is successful (Kampwirth & Powers, 2012). When discussing the issue of bullying with Ms. Stroll, I asked her which was more prevalent: physical or verbal instances of bullying. She indicated that both were a problem, so we agreed to focus on both. I indicated to her that bullying is something that is a serious issue within schools, so when establishing an acceptable frequency and intensity level for the behavior, we would want to make sure that we are being realistic for what desirable levels we would expect for bullying behaviors. We both agreed that there should be zero instances of bullying within the classroom. Thus, we decided that we would monitor baseline levels to gain a better idea of how often these instances of bullying occur and how serious they are. We decided to categorize them into physical and verbal forms. We came up with a list of examples for when we would be measuring these occurrences to ensure that there were specific observable and measurable behaviors. I created a sheet that would make it easy for Ms. Stroll to use event recording to track the daily occurrences of these behaviors. Ms. Stroll was asked to collect 4–5 days of consecutive baseline data so we could evaluate them. Baseline data indicated that there were at least four instances of verbal bullying and three instances of physical bullying during baseline data collection. This indicated to us that it was enough of a problem to go ahead and start implementing an intervention to help remediate the problem.

Intervention Design and Planning: Selection and Intervention Details

For the bullying intervention, I researched a variety of methods we could use and made copies of them to discuss with Ms. Stroll. After consulting with Ms. Stroll several times and observing her classroom, I had a better idea of the types of interventions that I felt would be most effective in her classroom. I specifically searched for interventions that minimized her time and effort for data collection, implementation, and maintenance. I knew that I would need to come up with easy ways for her to track things and make it easy for her to implement and monitor the intervention on her own, as she admitted to having an overwhelming workload and felt that behavior disruptions would make it difficult to implement and track intervention progress. I came up with a variety of techniques, but the most attractive to her was the Mystery Motivator. Therefore, I took some time to develop 5 weeks of Mystery Motivator sheets and behavior tracking sheets. I gave her pages of ideas to use as rewards and reinforcements for the class. I created an envelope that had the words "Stop Bullying" in an attractive red font outlined in black. I asked her to hang the envelope with the prize that she wrote on the tags next to the Mystery Motivator sheets. The class was first and second graders, so I explained to Ms. Stroll that it would be important to provide more regular attempts to receive the Mystery Motivator than for older children. Thus, I created the sheets to have reward opportunities for 4 out of the 5 days for Weeks 1 and 2. I then told her that for Week 3, I dropped it down to three and that for the fourth and fifth weeks, there would be two opportunities. I did this so that we could fade the reinforcements and see if the intervention was still effective despite the decrease in possible reward opportunities. Ms. Stroll agreed that this was a good idea. I gave her an activity sheet that I copied from *The Tough Kid Book: Practical Classroom Management Strategies* (Rhode, Jenson, & Reavis, 1992) so that she could take time to read it through and make sure that she was implementing the intervention correctly in case she forgot after our consult. I asked her to keep track of instances on one of the data sheets I created and to save the Mystery Motivator sheets so I could also use them to monitor more specifically what days the students did or did not receive their rewards.

Intervention Implementation: Intervention Is Delivered and Treatment Integrity Is Monitored

I met with Ms. Stroll to drop off all the materials and explain the intervention again. She gave me her attention, but it was as she was yelling and trying to correct her kids during a gym class lesson that took part in the classroom. She assured me that she was following everything I was saying as I explained the interventions to her. She was to begin implementing the intervention the following Monday. Data would only be collected for 4 days that week due to Friday being the start of spring break. There would be a lapse in data for the following week due to spring break, but the intervention would resume on Monday after spring break.

I was quite worried about the implementation of the intervention because I did not have Ms. Stroll's full attention when trying to explain the intervention to her. Although I made it easy, I wanted to make sure that she was carrying out the intervention in the thorough order and manner that we had discussed. I tried to e-mail and text Ms. Stroll to set up a time to come and see how the intervention was proceeding, but my diligent requests were ignored for some time. I finally told her that

I had to come in and pick up the data to try to force her to meet with me so I could see how the intervention was going. She tried to immediately push it out a week. I told her that we needed to meet within the next 2 days. She finally responded and asked me to give her 3 days so that she could put the data together for me. She then told me that she forgot to get it going during the first week but later remembered. As noted in Noell, Duhon, Gatti, and Connell (2002), integrity checks are an important component of data review and performance feedback sessions.

In terms of the treatment integrity, Ms. Stroll did not carry out the steps of the intervention effectively. She did not document instances of bullying as soon as they happened. She was supposed to let the class know that they were losing the Mystery Motivator for the day as soon as the instance of bullying occurred so that it would not occur in the future. She admitted that she often forgot to do the checklist at the end of the day with them to go over whether or not they earned the Mystery Motivator. She lacked excitement when introducing and reminding the kids of their chance to earn a Mystery Motivator. I asked her to keep the Mystery Motivator sheets so that I could see what days they earned rewards and compare these sheets with the tallies that she was keeping for instances of the type of bullying that was occurring and how often. When I wasn't there, I had no evidence that she was even doing the intervention at all other than what she was telling me, because I did not see the sheets. I was in on a Wednesday and saw that all five boxes were still covered up, but she didn't have instances of bullying for Monday or Tuesday. I asked her if the students had earned their Mystery Motivator since they had had no instances of bullying, and she told me that bullying had occurred but that she had just forgotten to mark it down. She did not carry out one step of this intervention according to what we had discussed. At one point, she told me that she was giving the students a chance at a weekly motivator prize when we discussed that kids that young would need daily reinforcement. I'm not sure the kids even got to see how this works at all, because every time I was in to see them do it, Ms. Stroll said that bullying had occurred that day, so the students did not earn a reward.

Evaluation

Ms. Stroll finally agreed to meet with me several weeks after the implementation of the intervention. We talked about the intervention and how she felt it was going. She told me that she did have to refer back to her sheets telling her how to carry out the intervention because she forgot. She originally indicated to me that she was giving the class weekly rewards if there were zero attempts all week. This was not what we originally discussed, so instead of telling her and accusing her of performing the intervention incorrectly, I explained to her that we should do daily reinforcement to see if we could improve and reduce the number of bullying incidences.

At this point, the intervention looked like it had been successful in reducing the number of bullying incidences. However, after looking over the data sheets and talking with Ms. Stroll, there was much reason to speculate that the intervention had not been carried out the way in which it was intended. Therefore, the integrity of the data had been compromised and required further evaluation of the intervention. At one of our consultation sessions close to the end, I explained to Ms. Stroll the importance of carrying out all necessary steps of the intervention and tracking daily progress. She, too, agreed that this was important; she just doesn't always do it this way and instead marks down data points when she remembers or allows them the reward opportunity the next day if she has forgotten to do this. I first explained to her that it is a very difficult process sometimes, but she is doing a great job. I then went on to discuss with her some of the reasons that we need to be systematically carrying out and documenting the data of the intervention every day. I told her that if we are not consistent, we may compromise the integrity and effectiveness for the Mystery Motivator to work in the future because we are not being consistent with the guidelines we established in the beginning, so the students are not sure which or when actions are being rewarded or punished. We re-established some new guidelines, and I told her that if at any point in time she was not able to carry out the intervention in an effective manner, we needed to regroup and discuss it from there.

Closure

Ms. Stroll agreed to carry out the intervention for 3 more weeks after our discussion regarding successful implementation and integrity of the intervention. Despite numerous attempts to get in touch with her, she still exhibited delayed or lack of response and follow-up. Without observable, measurable data, it was difficult to collaborate with Ms. Stroll regarding concerns or tweaks that may have been easy fixes for making the data tracking and implementation of the intervention successful.

Diversity Issues

Going into the consultation process, I almost expected there to be an issue of diversity that would present problems during the process, with Ms. Stroll being a Black, non-Hispanic female and myself being a White, non-Hispanic female. While identity development typically is not the focus of consultation, we must understand that saliency of one's identity in the perception of the consultee or consultant has the ability to influence the consultation process. Being able to understand the identity and experiences of one another or finding a common shared interest in some aspect of identity with the consultee allows opportunities for more effective consultation or enhanced outcomes (Ingraham, 2000). Of course, there were obvious differences in ethnicity, but I felt that we were able to bridge these differences through shared experiences for building effective communication and relationships within the consultation process.

I thought that another issue would come from her being resistant to me as a student attempting to consult with her. Surprisingly, to my disbelief, I felt as if she viewed me as a professional consultant who was there to tell her what to do to "fix" the problems she was experiencing within her classroom. She relied on me as the expert and was allowing me to make most of the decisions. After some time had passed, I realized that she was minimally providing insight for how she would like to approach and implement the intervention because she felt that I had more knowledge regarding the situation than I did. This hampered what I thought would be a true collaboration process. Whether it did or not wasn't the way that I wanted to proceed, so I started to say things to her like "I am just guessing here, you know your class better than I do" or "You know what types of rewards are interesting to them" because I wanted the consultation process to be a collaborative effort. One issue of diversity that I felt was present was what seemed to be the teacher's inability to view the students, the school, and the community within a cultural context. Comments that she made during consultation sessions about the students and/or the surrounding community were often negative. I rarely heard her speak in an empathic manner about her students. I was hoping to get her to see the students' behavior within a cultural context, which potentially would influence the intervention that we eventually would implement. Through consultation, I was able to help her understand that some of her original expectations may have been too strict and that she would never see improvement if she did not consider the cultural context of her culturally diverse classroom (Ingraham, 2000). It was important to help her understand the cultural issues in the school and neighborhood that might be contributing factors to the occurrence of problem behaviors in the classroom as well as to her students' current level of functioning in order to develop realistic goals so that they could experience success. I now realize that I had certain expectations because she was African American in terms of her understanding the students in her classroom. As suggested by Ingraham (2000), I considered that the racial similarity of the consultee and her students may have caused her to overcompensate by being more demanding of her students to demonstrate that there was no cultural favoritism.

Lessons Learned

Gutkin and Conoley (1990) explain that in order to serve children effectively, we must concentrate our attention and professional expertise on adults. One of the most important things I learned over the course of this process is that you have to put a lot of trust in the teacher to consistently carry out the interventions according to the specific guidelines the two of you have created. Although the teacher may say that he or she is carrying out the intervention accordingly, the more you talk about the intervention, the more detail you get, and you may realize it was not carried out the way it was intended. The next big lesson I learned is that when trying to be accommodating about when you intend to show up actually gives the consultee chances to get out of meeting with you. As I learned, this also allowed Ms. Stroll time to scramble to get data or possibly make up intervention data. Part of the consultation process was that we touch base with our consultee on a weekly basis. At those sessions, we were to review data. I now can see why weekly follow-ups are important. Noell et al. (2002) found that teachers did not maintain accurate implementation in the absence of programmed follow-up. I also recognize that being an outside consultant and not being in the school was a contributing factor, as I was not readily available and was reliant on appointment meetings rather than drop-in sessions, which would have been more likely to occur if I were in the building.

Another lesson learned is that sometimes it is possible that teachers indicate problems that perhaps are not generally problematic due to preconceived cultural or diversity bias or even perhaps the ability to isolate or conceptualize the "real" problem. When we first discussed the instances of bullying, Ms. Stroll indicated that this happened all the time. When asked after baseline data collection if the bullying incidences on any given week were more or less frequent than those gathered during baseline, she indicated that during baseline collection there seemed to be a few more incidences of bullying than normal. This is a good example, though, of an instance where you don't want to dismiss a teacher's concerns but rather want to address them and allow the teacher to discern if these truly are problematic behaviors.

As I reflect on the case, another takeaway is that poor classroom management is the basis for many behavior problems. Children need consistency and structure. I did not see evidence of this in Ms. Stroll's classroom during my visits. We talked about this in relation to the transition intervention because it was more relevant. In my opinion, her poor classroom management was contributing to a large portion of the transition problems and behavior problems we had been discussing. I would repeatedly watch her reprimand students and send them to the office as a means to try to gain control and authority over the class. Well-respected teachers within urban schools are able to successfully manage their classrooms instead of creating highly structured, punitive measures as an attempt to gain control (Ullucci, 2009).

Lastly, I learned that even though she was African American, she didn't appear to connect to her predominantly African American classroom of students as I thought she would. Thus, simply being from the same racial or ethnic group does not necessarily mean that you will automatically connect with others in a positive way. It could very well be that social class issues were a barrier to Ms. Stroll building successful relationships with her students. I had the good fortune to observe other classrooms with both African American and White teachers who appeared to be culturally connected to their students, which resulted in positive relationships between the teacher and the students. Ms. Stroll also failed to see how her lack of classroom management may have contributed to the behaviors she was seeing in her classroom despite the fact that she admitted to being overwhelmed, complained of having a heavy workload, and indicated that behavior disruptions might make it problematic to implement the intervention. While the consultation did not go exactly as planned, I do think that I was able to bring to her attention classroom management strategies that were not working and help her think about how she could possibly use interventions to effect behavioral change in students. I do have many takeaways that I hope will benefit me in future consultation cases.

As a novice consultant, I don't feel as if I had the skills necessary to move the consultee to where we needed to go. If I were doing it now, I would do it differently. I would really work with the consultee to define the problem from a more ecological perspective and only focus on one problem. She had a tendency to list numerous problems and wanted to focus a little bit on everything, hoping for measurable change. Time would have been better served being more focused on just one problem or instance of a larger concern. The inability to focus on one problem in hindsight probably made it more difficult to track data, which may have contributed to a failed intervention. I would also work on communication skills that would have allowed us to better conceptualize the concerns while at the same time allowing us to coincidentally address Ms. Stroll's lack of objectivity at times with her students. Finally, I realize now that I should have just dropped in to follow up with Ms. Stroll instead of trying to create regularly scheduled appointments so I could monitor the integrity of the intervention more closely and immediately fix instances where the intervention was not being carried out accordingly. This would have possibly allowed for more time to build a collaborative relationship with Ms. Stoll, which is essential for successful consultation.

Questions for Reflection

- In what ways could you have gotten the consultee to address or work past personal biases and generalizations?
- How can you bridge and establish connections to create a frame of reference with a consultee?
- What do you think would be the best way to proceed if you recognize that the intervention is compromised, is not being carried out accordingly, or perhaps data are being made up?

References

Gutkin, T. B., & Conoley, J. C. (1990). Reconceptualizing school psychology from a service delivery perspective: Implications for practice, training, and research. *Journal of School Psychology, 28*, 203–223.

Ingraham, C. L. (2000). Consultation through a multicultural lens: Multicultural and cross-cultural consultation in schools. *School Psychology Review, 29*, 320–343.

Kampwirth, T. J., & Powers, K. M. (2012). *Collaborative consultation in the schools: Effective practices for students with learning and behavior problems.* 4th Edition, Upper Saddle River, NJ: Pearson.

McCurdy, B.L., Mannella, M.C., & Eldridge, N. (2003). Positive behavior support in urban schools: Can we prevent the escalation of antisocial behavior? *Journal of Positive Behavior Interventions, 5*, 158–170.

Newman, D., Ingraham, C., & Shriberg, D. (2015). Consultee-centered consultation in contemporary schools. *NASP Communiqué, 42*, 14–16.

Noell, G.H., Duhon, G.J., Gatti, S.L., & Connell, J. E. (2002). Consultation, follow-up, and implementation of behavior management interventions in general education. *School Psychology Review, 31*, 217–234.

Rathvon, N. (2008). *Effective school interventions: Evidence-based strategies for improving student outcomes*. New York: Guilford Press.

Rhode, G., Jenson, W.R., & Reavis, H.K. (1992). *The tough kid book: Practical classroom management strategies*. Longmont, CO: Sopris West.

Ullucci, K. (2009). "This has to be family": Humanizing classroom management in urban schools. *Journal of Classroom Interaction, 44*, 13–28.

PART III

Consultation Within the Cultural Context of Poverty, Race, and School

6

THE PROBLEMS ASSOCIATED WITH VIEWING STUDENTS THROUGH A DEFICIT LENS

Naima Shirdon

Advance Organizer Questions

- How can a teacher's cultural bias impact his or her approach to teaching, classroom discipline, and behavioral interventions?
- How might issues like staff morale and cohesion impact classroom dynamics?
- What are some of the challenges that this case presents, and what skills would aid a novice consultant in navigating these concerns?

School Culture

School culture encompasses the values, traditions, beliefs, and policies within a school that can be shaped and advanced by a school's principal and teacher leaders (Short & Greer, 1997). It is heavily informed by the nature of collegiality within the school and the extent to which staff feel included and appreciated. Although these factors are central to school staff carrying out their roles effectively, they often go unaddressed as schools prioritize more immediate and perhaps visible issues. As such, communication can suffer, and teachers may also feel alienated. In situations such as these, a lack of a crucial sense of belonging and collegiality may have wide-reaching effects—perhaps negatively influencing teacher motivation and, ultimately, teaching practices in the classroom setting. Considering the dynamics of school culture enabled me to enter the consultant–consultee relationship with the understanding that factors external to the classroom setting play an important role. School culture can significantly shape a teacher's sense of self and even make her question her place within the school.

As a first-year doctoral student, while studying aspects of collaborative consultation in schools, I had the opportunity to engage in a consultation relationship with an elementary school teacher and put the theories and concepts we had learned into practice as a novice consultant. The immediate goals of the consultation were to facilitate the implementation of a behavioral intervention. The school in question was a K–5 elementary lottery school that offered a teacher-directed curriculum. Due to the fact that it was a lottery school, the students hailed from many different neighborhoods.

Demographics

At the time of this consultation, the school was being renovated and therefore was housed in a school about a mile from the original school but in the same community. This school building did not have its own population but was being used as a swing space as schools throughout the district were undergoing renovation or getting a new building. Both buildings are in a historic district of a major metropolitan Midwestern city, with the original school building sitting in the heart of that community. What is interesting is that the population in the school building does not reflect the community, which is well off and predominantly White. According to the state report card, 78.3% of the students were economically disadvantaged, which illustrates the level of poverty that enveloped their respective neighborhoods. Moreover, the school had a classification of continuous improvement, indicating that it met 4 out of the 8 potential measures and had room to grow. The number of enrolled students amounted to 274; of those students, 84.5% were Black, 7.2% were White, 6.9% were Multiracial, and 6.4% had disabilities. Furthermore, the students wore red, white, and blue uniforms, which is a testament to the patriotic emphasis the school had, along with an eagle mascot.

The Role of the Principal

It is when we delve beyond the demographics and explore the inner workings of the school that the problems that plagued this elementary school become evident. In their book *Collaborative Consultation in the Schools*, Kampwirth and Powers (2012) mention that "student difficulties do not only reside within the students themselves or because of the nature of their classrooms or homes" (p. 228). Greater factors such as school culture and decisions on a systems level have profound effects upon the effectiveness of teachers and the resultant output of the students. It is often the principal who is associated with establishing and developing school culture and ultimately contributing to the growth of the school. A principal's failure to set the agenda and work toward creating a cohesive school culture allows many other facets of the school to suffer. In contrast, principals who focus on creating a positive school culture are able to achieve wide-reaching outcomes; in these settings, teachers feel confident and appreciated and engage in professional development, students are valued, and parental input is sought (Habegger, 2008).

The principal at the school, Mrs. Owens, was fairly new, having started at the school in a rapid and unexpected fashion 2 years ago. It appeared that the staff (particularly veteran staff) were initially skeptical about Mrs. Owens upon her arrival, and the feeling of a lack of trust persisted. Furthermore, this was compounded by the fact that aspects such as academics and discipline seemed to represent more immediate concerns for Mrs. Owens; as such, a culture was created that did not seem to emphasize relationship building or schoolwide communication.

Staff Dynamics

Regarding the nature of staff relationships, Mrs. Brown—the teacher I consulted with—shared that the staff morale was very low and that the school did not boast a supportive environment. Her descriptions of the school were most telling when she juxtaposed them with the other elementary school where she spent half the week teaching music. Although both schools served similar populations, she drew key differences between the schools. She mentioned that while the teachers at the other school may get burned out, they support one another, are kind to each other, and there is an air of cooperation. Conversely, the staff morale at the lottery school is extremely low; the administration recently held a meeting in which all staff were invited to discuss the problems that exist. The importance of the open discussion approach to solving problems is alluded to in the following statement: "Change from above can be subtly if not overtly rejected by those closest to the problems because these individuals don't feel that they were a part of the problem solving process" (Kampwirth & Powers, 2012, p. 237). As such, the meeting was facilitated by the principal and involved staff discussing some elements of the book *The Five Dysfunctions of a Team*. Ironically, those teachers who were the catalyst for the meeting (which involved veteran teachers not feeling supported, gossiping, and expressing discontent about the overall politics of the school) were not present. This is very telling of the culture of the school, as it paints a picture of mistrust and a lack of support.

The issues of staff dynamics are even more so illustrated by Mrs. Brown's account of collegiality. As a new addition to the school, she found it odd that no teachers eat their lunch in the break room. Following the norm, she then began eating her lunch by herself in her classroom. Another source of isolation is the location of her music classroom, which—on the school's bottom floor—is isolated from much of the traffic of the school. Both aspects contribute to feelings of isolation and a lack of connectedness with staff members, indicating that the school lacks a cooperative and interconnected team dynamic. Mrs. Brown herself recognized that she was new to the school and may not know all of its inner workings, but she sensed that "something is not right." Overall, it is telling that although Mrs. Brown was at the school for just half the week and felt isolated while she was there, she could still sense an overall malaise that was greatly affecting the teachers.

Consultant and Consultee Relationship

The consultee, Mrs. Brown (a White female in her 30s), was a music teacher who initially came to the elementary school after being staff reduced out of a band program. Her predecessor left the school abruptly after the school year had started because she received a teaching position elsewhere (a metaphor, perhaps, for the greater instability that plagues the school). As a result, Mrs. Brown assumed her position in the school in the ninth week. At the start of the consultation process, she had been at the school for 16 weeks. She had only ever taught middle and high school students, so this was her first foray into teaching elementary school children. She described her transition as both smooth and difficult. She was charmed by the enthusiasm that the younger children exhibited, yet the job also brought with it increasing challenges. The difficulty stemmed from the fact that she was in two schools (attending one on Mondays through Wednesdays and the other on Thursdays and Fridays) and taught a total of 600 kids, making it difficult to remember their names. She also mentioned that she was new to the instrumental curriculum and was not familiar with the relevant area of child development, as she was used to working with older children.

These revelations, which she shared in our first meeting, truly set the tone for our consultative relationship. Our apparent differences did not hinder the nature of the consultation. In some situations, novice consultants may be met with resistance, given their junior status in relation to a veteran teacher. However, as a first-year doctoral student and a Somali American, my positionality did not seem to hinder the development of our relationship or make Mrs. Brown reticent to share her candid opinions. We enjoyed an honest and open relationship; there was an air of comfort, and Mrs. Brown was always very giving and thorough with her answers. She was an active participant in the discussion. She did not simply passively accept suggestions; instead, she thought critically about them and asked questions, which was an indication that she was thinking about how the plan would be actualized. I was always sure to ask for her input and thoughts on the intervention throughout the process to ensure that she understood it and felt that it was feasible. These elements combined to make for a good working relationship. I believe that this was also facilitated by my use of communication skills.

Communication Skills

For a novice consultant, one of the main pitfalls of the interviewing process while consulting is adhering rigidly to a series of questions that you craft ahead of the interview and not adapting to the natural course of the conversation. Doing so leads the novice consultant to not fully engage in active listening, instead becoming preoccupied with the next question on his or her list. I was keen to avoid this dynamic, as it can prevent the formation of a meaningful relationship and lead to structured and formal interviewing. Instead, I sought to have our sessions mirror an organic conversation, in which I was attuned to opportunities to request more information and explore the nuances of Mrs. Brown's situation. I found that our consultation interviews flowed well in that I used Mrs. Brown's responses to guide the interview, not adhering to a set of questions, but instead allowing the interview to take its course. Her responses would also lead to more probing questions as well as clarification statements to ensure that I had understood her correctly. There was a balance of both closed and open questions, the latter providing more opportunities for Mrs. Brown to actively engage. My body language and nonverbal communication displayed that I was attending and actively listening; I would often nod as she spoke, saying "Right" or "Okay," which communicated understanding, and would also maintain eye contact. I believe that this body language aided Mrs. Brown's perception of me, in that I did not come across as rigid or excessively formal. I believe that she felt comfortable and did not feel threatened by my questions. This perception was also strengthened by my empathic statements when she spoke of her difficulties.

The importance of communicating support and encouragement cannot be underscored in the consultative relationship, particularly in a situation where the consultee feels isolated from her peers. Communication is a tool through which consultants can show that they care for, respect, and appreciate the consultee and are thus truly invested in a successful outcome for all parties involved. I was intentional about showing my appreciation for Mrs. Brown's insights as we negotiated a plan of action, as well as her subsequent efforts to carry out the intervention. This also served to further the collaborative dimension of the consultation, as it reinforced that this was a team effort.

It would seem that open communication and developing a meaningful relationship are truly the bedrock for effective consultation. If there is an atmosphere of trust, the consultee can be more candid and get to the heart of the matter while also remaining practical about what he or she can and cannot do throughout the course of the intervention as it relates to his or her particular circumstances. Employing messages of support and appreciation paved the way for open and honest dialogue.

Problem-Solving Process

The problem-solving process incorporates four distinct steps: (a) identify the problem, (b) develop an intervention plan, (c) implement the intervention plan, and (d) evaluate the effectiveness of the plan. This process guided our consultative relationship and gave it structure and purpose. The following is an analysis of each step of the problem-solving process.

Problem Identification

During our initial interview, I was able to get a sense of the target problem that Mrs. Brown wished to tackle. The problem was that the transition time to get all the choir students from their fourth- and fifth-grade classrooms down to the choir classroom (which is on the bottom floor) was very lengthy and cut into potential choir time. The goal was to reduce the transition time of gathering all the students from their classrooms to settling into the choir classroom to an acceptable level. The goal of the week would be gradually lowered and informed by students' achievement on past timings.

In order to verify the problem behavior and take a baseline measure, I observed the transition time of the fourth-grade class. The baseline measure, which I timed myself during observation, amounted to 12 min. This included the time it took for Mrs. Brown to retrieve the students from their classrooms (which were on different floors) and return to the classroom. The timing was stopped when the students were in their seats and ready for instruction.

I also had the opportunity to observe Mrs. Brown interacting with her students in the classroom setting and was thus able to gain an understanding of her classroom management techniques and her relationships with her students. Her interactions with her students seemed to display a lack of caring and respect; she seemed to anticipate misbehavior from her students and at the first sign of it would respond—perhaps disproportionately—by raising her voice to address them. In one case, Mrs. Brown called out a student who had been speaking and did not give him a chance to explain himself; instead, she interrupted him and simply attempted to silence him. This dynamic also was not helped by the fact that she initially called the student in question by the wrong name and was corrected by his peers. Conveying respect and caring is central to developing meaningful relationships with students, which is considered by some researchers to be the very foundation for a student's academic success (Erickson, 1987). Moreover, case studies on urban schools have juxtaposed turbulent school culture alongside students expressing sentiments that their teachers do not seem to trust or care for them (Mirón & Lauria, 1998). Ultimately, the relationships that teachers develop with students—and by extension their classroom management techniques—are in part informed by their understanding of their students' home lives. If teachers lack understanding of their students' backgrounds and communities, this may lead to forming assumptions, which may hinder meaningful relationship development. My observations of Mrs. Brown's interactions with her students alluded to her own biases about the communities that they came from (this is explored later in the chapter).

Although it became clear that Mrs. Brown could benefit from a larger scale classroom management intervention, the chosen intervention focused on one aspect of classroom management (transitions) that Mrs. Brown targeted for reduction. Due to the fact that she suggested this direction for the intervention, she was invested in a successful outcome.

Intervention Design and Planning

From the information I had collected from Mrs. Brown regarding the problem, it was decided that a transition intervention would be put in place to reduce the students' transition time. An AB design would be utilized—that is, a two-phase design consisting of the baseline phase and the intervention phase. Essentially, the basic idea would be that each week, there would be a goal for the transition time that the students would have to meet in order to earn activity time at the end of class. It incorporated both token economy and Mystery Motivator concepts—the former insofar as being able to earn activities at the end of class and the latter insofar as picking the activity of the day out of a bowl. The following is a script I gave to Mrs. Brown to facilitate introducing the intervention:

> Today we're going to talk about an exciting way that we can earn points by playing a game at the end of class. Right now, it takes a pretty long time for us to gather all of you from your classrooms to get down to choir. We're going to try to reduce that time. Starting now, I'll be timing how long it takes to get all the students from their classrooms down to choir. But it's not just about how fast we go; what are some other rules you think we should have? What do you think would help make the time shorter? [*Here's where you would take down responses on the board. You might prompt them with other questions here to get them to bring up other rules. Hopefully the more they're involved in the process of making up the rules, the more likely they are to remember and abide by them.*]

Rules

1. Getting to choir in a reduced time
2. Timing will be stopped once everyone is sitting in their seat and ready for class
3. Not talking in line
4. Being in a straight and orderly line
5. Listening to Mrs. Brown

> Each week, we will have a goal of the number of minutes it should take us to get down to choir. After I take the timing, we will write it down on this poster here and if it is less than our goal for the week, we get to have an activity toward the end of class. You will pick a piece of paper out of this bowl here to tell us what activity we will have for the day. [*Also, you can announce the goal for next week.*]

The following are the chronological steps of the intervention that were given to Mrs. Brown to adhere to:

1. Time the students for each transition (from how long it takes to get them all to choir to how long it takes for them to settle down in their seats and for you to begin your lesson).
2. Remind the students while getting them from their classroom that they are working toward the activity at the end of class today and to remember what the rules are.
3. Once you get back to class, announce the timing, write it down on the poster board, and let them know if they will or won't be getting the activity at the end of the day.

   a. The poster board can incorporate the following columns: Goal of the Week, Timing, and Activity.

4. Ask students if their timing is under the goal for the week.

   a. Consider having a student write the check mark if the activity is earned.

5. If the goal is met, have a student pick a paper out of a bowl of papers that outline different activities the class could engage in for the day and engage in the activity for the last 10 min.

Due to the initial baseline of 12 min, a goal of 10 min was set for the first week. Outlining the details of the intervention was a collective process insofar as Mrs. Brown giving me feedback and thinking through processes to see if they were applicable to her classroom (e.g., the types of activities that were suggested). Early on in our discussion, Mrs. Brown was eager to set some rules, as "it's not just about how fast the kids are, but also about getting to class in an orderly way." Here, I encouraged her to query the classroom on what they thought the rules should look like to help reduce transition time. This harkens back to Ullucci's (2009) "Humanizing Classroom Management, in Urban Schools," a journal article that emphasizes creating "caring communities" within the classroom. A manifestation of this would be the teacher communicating respect to her students. When we restore students' dignity and show them that we truly care, it follows that the teacher–student relationship would also be strengthened. As such, the students in the choir classroom were able to have a sense of ownership when Mrs. Brown solicited rules from the group, which would also raise their level of investment in the intervention. The same is also true for Mrs. Brown; as planning the intervention was collaborative, this also allowed her to have a sense of ownership over it.

Intervention Implementation

Implementing the intervention proved to be more difficult than I had anticipated. This phase in the process was met with many challenges. These challenges were due in part to the infrequency with which the choir class meets (only once a week), as well as external school factors. To illustrate, the week after we had finalized the intervention, Mrs. Brown was to introduce it to the class as a whole. She also decided that this would be a good opportunity to take another baseline measure. Neither of these intentions was carried out as planned. In one case, one of the fifth-grade teachers was absent and there was no substitute. When this happens, those students are split up among five or six other teachers. Therefore, all the children were scattered all over the building. To complicate matters, some teachers took their students outside due to the nice weather. Because Mrs. Brown had to scour the school to find her students, it took her 15 min to gather only half of the class. She introduced the intervention, though half of the class was not present, so we had to introduce the intervention to the other students through other means (Mrs. Brown spoke with all the classes that had the choir students to inform them of the intervention).

When the day finally arrived to implement the intervention and take the initial data, this ended up taking 14 min (which exceeded the baseline) due to other special circumstances. Out of four of the teachers from whom she retrieved her choir students, two of them had substitutes who weren't anticipating the students being taken out for choir. This required Mrs. Brown to explain the process to the substitutes on both occasions, which greatly increased their timing. Thus, the students did not meet the goal for the week and were not awarded with the activity at the day's end. The treatment integrity check yielded that Mrs. Brown had followed all of the required steps of the intervention; however, one cannot account for such unanticipated variables.

Evaluation

Mrs. Brown offered that she believed that the intervention itself was good and that the students were motivated by the concept of an activity at the day's end; however, it was the external factors that proved to be difficult for the successful application of the intervention.

Closure

The final sentiments that Mrs. Brown shared with me were telling: during our last meeting, she mentioned how helpful it would be to have some sort of class (potentially at the local university) that explores interventions for different populations that would give teachers the resources to be more successful with classroom management. Giving them this toolbox would make teachers feel a lot more competent, as opposed to having their efforts flippantly dismissed by someone saying "Well, you just don't have classroom management skills." Those who are organizing professional development and people at the higher level "aren't willing to be real" about the problems that exist. I did not get the sense that Mrs. Brown was referring to the principal here—who, despite opposition from veteran staff, she described as kind and hardworking—but perhaps those operating at a higher administrator level.

It also did not seem as if Mrs. Brown was simply seeking generic classroom management tips, but more so trying to understand how classroom management relates to the diverse populations she works with—the confluence of diversity and effective interventions. Mrs. Brown's frustrations about the lack of relevant professional development mirrors the literature that contends that professional development, for the most part, does not help teachers understand their students in terms of their communities and home lives (Sleeter, 1992). It is critically important for a teacher to understand both his or her own culture as well as the culture of his or her students in order to engage in culturally relevant pedagogy (Ladson-Billings, 1995). Employing this approach emphasizes student–teacher relationships and ultimately contributes to the development of effective teaching methods and more appropriate classroom management techniques.

Diversity Issues

While Mrs. Brown had experience working in urban schools and was thus familiar with the reality of the school's student body and their surrounding community, she still seemed to hold beliefs that hindered her from developing the mind-set of an effective teacher (a concept that is explored by Goldstein & Brooks, 2007). One of the ideas that an effective teacher adheres to is that all students wish to be successful. Mrs. Brown, however, expressed on more than one occasion that certain students do not want to learn. By extension, she also mentioned that certain children (presumably those with behavioral concerns) come from families where education is not valued and women are not respected. It is clear, then, that Mrs. Brown seems to view her students from a cultural deficit perspective—the notion that the problem lies with the student themselves and their cultural background and community. This mind-set also externalizes the problem—believing that a student's failings are solely due to the communities from which he or she comes takes away the culpability on the part of the teacher. Furthermore, adhering to a deficit mind-set may have informed the problematic nature of Mrs. Brown's interactions with her students, principally that she appeared to display a lack of caring and respect. Being able to explore one's views about the students one works with and how those views are represented in one's teaching and student engagement is a vital step in implementing culturally relevant pedagogy.

In contrast to the deficit model, Goldstein and Brooks (2007) illustrate the mind-set of an effective teacher: "If the student is not learning, educators must ask how they can adapt their teaching style and instructional material to meet student needs" (p. 191). Doing so will allow the teacher to focus on what is in his or her control and how he or she can benefit his or her class by taking into account the students' individual agency and incorporating this into instruction. Thus, the importance of having an understanding of where the children are coming from—that is, a truthful and meaningful understanding—will increase the teacher's empathy, facilitating viewing students in a more comprehensive manner rather than simply assigning generalizations to those children whose behaviors may be more difficult to manage. The development of empathy also has greater implications for classroom behavior, as it can increase trust and thus affect behavior by adopting the relational approach to discipline (Ripski & Gregory, 2008).

Lessons Learned

The opportunity to participate in this consultative relationship and work through the problem-solving model enabled me to apply what I had learned about in class and made for a rich learning experience. As this was my first foray into consultation, I learned that I truly enjoy the process of collaborative consultation—in particular, developing a meaningful relationship with Mrs. Brown and working with her to both identify the problem and formulate a targeted plan. I also learned of the nuances of consultation and aspects to watch out for to ensure that you have the other party's buy-in. This includes looking for whether or not they critically consider the suggestions you put forth by asking questions or making statements that show they are thinking about how the intervention will be implemented in the classroom. Passive agreement, even if it is accompanied by excitement, may suggest that the other party is a willing participant, but it underscores the fact that they may not be thinking about the intervention's practical application as it relates to their classroom and that they are also not truly engaged in a collaborative engagement. My consultative relationship with Mrs. Brown had the elements of active participation and critical questions, which made it truly collaborative. This also helped Mrs. Brown have a sense of ownership over the intervention.

Beyond the obvious challenges that I had anticipated (difficulty obtaining a good amount of data due to the infrequency of choir class and scheduling conflicts contributing to a lack of opportunities to observe the transitions), I was more surprised by the external factors that I had not accounted for, which played a major role in the failure of the intervention. The frequency of substitute teachers and, in the event that no substitute could be found, dividing a class into multiple classrooms was significant. It not only had the effect of hindering a successful intervention insofar as increasing the timing of the transitions, but there was also the added component of increasing behavior concerns. Mrs. Brown mentioned that the students depend on the stability of the classroom: "When there is any change in their regular routine, they can't handle it." Essentially, the students had a hard time adjusting to unanticipated changes and needed to have structure—they relied on it. This was made more salient by the fact that teacher absences occurred with seeming regularity. When I asked Mrs. Brown why she thought this was, she said that it was easy to get burned out by the children, so some teachers take a day off or a few days off. This phenomenon is further informed by school culture and the lack of support and low morale that plagues the staff. It is complemented by the prominent study on teacher absenteeism conducted by Steers and Rhodes (1978), which asserts that absenteeism is primarily influenced by job satisfaction and is also heavily impacted by organizational practices, school culture, and employee attitudes and values. Thus, it is important to consider how external factors, influenced by overall school culture, may affect the efficacy of a behavioral intervention.

While external factors played a main role in contributing to the failure of the intervention, one would be remiss not to discuss the significance of diversity in this case. Throughout the course of the intervention, Mrs. Brown displayed growth in assessing her classroom management difficulties. Initially, she seemed to solely blame the students, citing the values and beliefs of their communities as a hindrance to their academic and classroom success. However, during the closure phase of our consultation, she expressed interest in attending a training that would give her insight into her students' diverse backgrounds and how she can be more effective with classroom management given this understanding. Her desire to receive diversity training displayed her progression in not simply attributing the problem to the student but instead thinking more globally and acknowledging her own role in ameliorating classroom dynamics. She correctly identified that her own lack of understanding of her students and their communities could contribute to some ineffective teaching and classroom management techniques.

As a consultant, I felt pleased that I was able to have an open dialogue about diversity with Mrs. Brown and that she was comfortable sharing both her honest opinions about her students and some of her own vulnerabilities as a teacher. I believe that the development of our relationship throughout the consultation (including active listening and remaining supportive) created an environment conducive to Mrs. Brown sharing her thoughts openly. In retrospect, when she shared an interest in diversity training, in the short term I could have offered her articles and materials that would have introduced her to helpful frameworks with which to view her students. The second component of the multicultural school consultation (MSC) framework, consultee learning and development, outlines key domains that aid the consultee in strengthening his or her teaching practice (Ingraham, 2000). In particular, the knowledge domain recognizes the need of the consultee to better understand the diverse populations he or she works with and acknowledges the supportive role the consultant would play in this regard. Articles such as "Toward a Conception of Culturally Responsive Classroom Management (CRCM)" vividly illustrate the need for multicultural competence as it relates to classroom management and outline what types of mistakes can occur when one does not fully understand the population one is working with

(Weinstein, Tomlinson-Clarke, & Curran, 2004). The authors principally mention that "CRCM is a frame of mind, more than a set of strategies or practices" (p. 27). I believe that a focus on culturally responsive classroom management would greatly help Mrs. Brown and her cohort in being more effective in the classroom.

Ultimately, this case study revealed the complex interplay between external factors, school culture, and diversity and how they may combine to impact both the implementation of a behavioral intervention and also undermine teaching practices. The school in question painted a picture of a disenfranchised and disconnected staff that frequently experienced burnout. It was also marked by a lack of stability due to regular teacher absenteeism. These aspects principally derailed the success of the intervention; however, diversity also played a main role in shaping teacher perspectives and informing teacher–student interactions and relationships. In order to foster meaningful relationships with students, teachers must be able to acknowledge and question their biases. They may also take the further step of trying to better understand their diverse student body in an effort to engage in culturally responsive teaching practices. As a consultant, being able to probe and support this process of teacher development is beneficial to strengthening both the consultee–consultant relationship and, perhaps more importantly, the teacher–student relationship (which is truly at the heart of good educational practice).

Questions for Reflection

- In what ways can the cultural deficit perspective manifest itself in the educational context?
- How might a consultant aid a teacher who appears to view his or her students through a deficit model? What perspectives or resources can be offered?
- What role does school culture play in impacting both staff and classroom dynamics?
- Communication and relationship building are at the heart of effective consultation. In what ways can a consultant show care and respect in an effort to build a meaningful relationship?

References

Erickson, F. (1987). Transformation and school success: The politics and culture of educational achievement. *Anthropology and Education Quarterly, 18*, 335–336.

Goldstein, S., & Brooks, R. B. (2007). *Understanding and managing children's classroom behavior* (2nd ed.). Hoboken, NJ: Wiley & Sons.

Habegger, S. (2008). The principal's role in successful schools: Creating a positive school culture. *Principal, 88*, 42–46.

Ingraham, C.L. (2000). Consultation through a multicultural lens: Multicultural and cross-cultural consultation in schools. *School Psychology Review, 29*, 320–343.

Kampwirth, T. J., & Powers, K. M. (2012). *Collaborative consultation in the schools* (4th ed.). Upper Saddle River, NJ: Pearson.

Ladson-Billings, G. (1995). Toward a theory of culturally relevant pedagogy. *American Educational Research Journal, 32*, 465–491.

Mirón, L. F., & Lauria, M. (1998). Student voice as agency: Resistance and accommodation in inner-city schools. *Anthropology and Education Quarterly, 29*, 189–213.

Ripski, M.B., & Gregory, A. (2008). Adolescent trust in teachers: Implications for behavior in the high school classroom. *School Psychology Review, 37*, 337–353.

Short, P. M., & Greer, J.T. (1997). *School leadership in empowered schools: Themes from innovative efforts*. Upper Saddle River, NJ: Simon & Schuster.

Sleeter, C. E. (1992). *Keepers of the American dream: A study of staff development and multicultural education*. Washington, DC: Falmer Press.

Steers, R. M., & Rhodes, S. R. (1978). Major influences on employee attendance: A process model. *Journal of Applied Psychology, 63*, 391–407.

Ullucci, K. (2009). "This has to be family": Humanizing classroom management in urban schools. *Journal of Classroom Interaction, 44*, 13–28.

Weinstein, C. S., Tomlinson-Clarke, S., & Curran, M. (2004). Toward a conception of culturally responsive classroom management. *Journal of Teacher Education, 55*, 25–38.

7

IMPROVING SELF-ESTEEM AND REDUCING FEMALE RELATIONAL AGGRESSION IN URBAN CLASSROOMS

Lauren Wargelin and McKenzie Mallen

Advance Organizer Questions

- What are the most important qualities of consultant–consultee relationships?
- How can explicit communication and effective questioning be implemented when working with consultees in the classroom?
- How can consultants ensure that teachers effectively implement interventions with integrity?

Case Overview

Our first case as novice consultants took place at Ackerman Elementary School working with two fifth-grade teachers, Ms. Miley and Ms. Smith. Both teachers shared concerns about relational aggression between female students in their classrooms. This included behaviors such as spreading rumors or lies, intentionally excluding peers, threatening to withdraw friendships, and stealing friends. This consultation case was an excellent learning experience for both of us as novice consultants. We will use this experience to continue to grow our consultation skills in the future.

School Culture

Ackerman Elementary School is located in an urban neighborhood in a large Midwestern city and is part of a large urban school district. Most of the students attending the school live in the surrounding area, which is characterized by high crime rates and poor living conditions. Ackerman Elementary houses preschool through fifth-grade students. The majority of the students are Black (89.6%) and receive free or reduced-price lunches (83.1%; Civil Rights Data Collection, 2011). Within the past 8 years, Ackerman has had five different principals. Within the past few years, the school was forced to reconstitute due to not meeting state standards of adequate yearly progress. During the reconstitution, approximately half of the teachers were let go and replaced. Therefore, at least half of the teachers are somewhat new to Ackerman.

Fortunately, the current principal, Ms. Thomas, is passionate about connecting with the community and has the determination to pull the school out of academic emergency. She is currently completing her third year at the school. She is young and energetic but also has high expectations for her teachers. We worked with two fifth-grade teachers at Ackerman Elementary. Both teachers were highly involved, demanding, and authoritative in their classrooms. Ms. Miley is an African American teacher who was in her first year at Ackerman Elementary but who had at least 10 years of teaching experience. Ms. Smith is a White teacher who had spent 20 of her 21 years as a teacher at Ackerman Elementary. Through observations and discussions, it was clear that both attempted to connect with their classrooms in a culturally appropriate way. However, there were some different classroom management styles between the two teachers. They both appeared to have an understanding of the broader context within which their students live, use culturally appropriate classroom management strategies, and have a commitment to building a caring classroom (Weinstein, Tomlinson-Clarke, & Curran, 2004). Overall, the staff at Ackerman Elementary appeared to be willing to do whatever it took to help their students reach their full potentials.

Consultant Roles

We originally began the consultation process at Ackerman Elementary working separately with two fifth-grade teachers. Our intentions were to guide our respective teachers in solving the biggest challenges in their classes. After meeting several times with our respective teachers to determine the nature of the classroom problems we would be tackling, we were updating each other about our consultation experiences thus far. During this conversation, we discovered that both teachers described the same problem: relational aggression of female students. Relational aggression is defined as the intent to harm a relationship between two or more individuals through social manipulation (Bradshaw, Sawyer, & O'Brennan, 2007). This includes behaviors such as spreading rumors or lies, intentionally excluding a peer, threatening to withdraw a friendship, and stealing friends. Furthermore, we realized that the two teachers shared two classes of students so that the entire fifth grade essentially functioned as one unit, completing the same work with the same teachers. In order to assist our consultees most effectively, we decided to work together to solve the problem in the fifth-grade classrooms. The teachers happily agreed, as collaborating meant increased consultant support and instructor consistency across classrooms. Together, the four of us determined that the best way to target female relational aggression was to foster positive classroom environments in two ways simultaneously: through classroom-wide interventions and by teaching relational skills in a pullout group that the female fifth graders could elect to join. We believed that this would both create a positive classroom climate and teach some of the skills that the female students were lacking. We will distinguish our unique experiences with our respective teachers throughout the duration of this chapter.

Consultant and Consultee Relationships

While each of us primarily worked with one particular teacher, we simultaneously built a relationship with the other consultant's teacher throughout the course of the consultation process. Lauren Wargelin primarily worked with Ms. Miley, and McKenzie Mallen primarily worked with Ms. Smith during the early stages of consultation. We are both White female students in our first year of graduate school.

Even though we were novice consultants, we found it relatively easy to establish collaborative relationships with both Ms. Miley and Ms. Smith. Ms. Miley was extremely open to the consultation process even though she had not participated in it before. Her willingness to try our new ideas demonstrated her strong desire to help her students. I (Wargelin) used rapport building as my primary method for cultivating a strong relationship with Ms. Miley. We talked about issues outside the focus of consultation, which showed her that I was interested in getting to know her and that I genuinely liked her. I tried to remember specific information she told me so that I could ask her about it the next time I saw her. For example, around the time we began consultation, Ms. Miley began leading Girls on the Run, a program to increase self-esteem and fitness in young women. I made sure to check in with her about how that was going when I saw her each week. Building rapport in this way helped me to build referent power in the consultation relationship (Kampwirth & Powers, 2012). Building referent power showed Ms. Miley that she could identify with me and trust me as a consultant.

Ms. Smith was also very open for discussion and easy to talk with. Through the same rapport building used with Ms. Miley, I (Mallen) developed a strong relationship with Ms. Smith. Ms. Smith demonstrated that she was fully engaged in her classroom and her students' success, as she expressed genuine concern for her students. This dedication made it easy for me to work with her. I showed empathy throughout our conversations about the difficulties that her fifth-grade class presented. Through information gathered from the initial interview, it was evident that Ms. Smith was invested in her classroom by her comments on how much she knew about each individual student, their families, and the community. This knowledge seemed to also be a result of her many years in the school. This made it easy to work with her because I could tell that she truly wanted to see positive change in her classroom. Both of the consultants and the consultees were willing to try new approaches in the classrooms even though we were not sure they would be effective. Our joint willingness and openness to try these new approaches in each classroom cultivated supportive, relaxed consultation relationships.

Communication Skills

Communication skills were essential for this consultation case because we were implementing both an intervention and a pullout group for girls (Girl Talk) in the classrooms. On top of the weekly Girl Talk meetings, we had to find time to ensure that the intervention plan was followed. Outside of the school, the majority of our communication was done through text messages, which was the consultees' preferred method due to its convenience. During our face-to-face meetings, we used established and effective communication skills such as attending, active listening, empathy, and questioning (Kampwirth & Powers, 2012).

Ms. Miley

Attending and actively listening to Ms. Miley showed her that I (Wargelin) heard her concerns and understood her point of view. This was my biggest strength in communication. I made sure to fully attend to Ms. Miley when we talked. I also clarified statements she made that were unclear, paraphrased the information she gave me, and summarized what we talked about at least once during the conversation.

Empathy was the area of communication that I struggled with the most. Though I felt empathetic toward Ms. Miley, I realized by watching my recordings of our consultation sessions that I often did not express it well. Leading Girl Talk helped me to better empathize with Ms. Miley. When she expressed her frustration or disbelief about the way her class was acting, I could relate what she was saying to my experiences working with her class. I understood the challenge of managing a classroom of fifth graders while remaining professional and composed. Over time, I learned to use empathy statements that expressed my understanding of Ms. Miley's frustration. Some of the empathy statements I used included phrases such as, "That is a tough situation," "I can see why you are stressed," and "That is so frustrating." Though expressing empathy felt excessive and insincere at first, I became more comfortable and developed this skill through practice.

Effective questioning helped me to gain a broader understanding of the problems in Ms. Miley's class. I used as many open-ended questions as possible in order to maximize the amount of information I could obtain. I noticed by watching videos of our consultation sessions that I occasionally asked multiple questions at a time. I worked to improve this throughout the consultation process in order to be clearer and to elicit more informative responses from Ms. Miley. I focused on only asking for one piece of information at once and then asking follow-up questions to obtain details.

Ms. Smith

The main reason my (Mallen's) relationship with Ms. Smith was successful was because of good communication skills. It was easy to be empathetic because Ms. Smith genuinely wanted to help her students. Being empathic is crucial in the consultation process because consultees want consultants to truly listen to their concerns and to understand them at a level greater than just the word meanings alone (Kampwirth & Powers, 2012). By relating Ms. Smith's concerns to my own experiences, I connected with her. We were both outside of the normative culture of the students at Ackerman, making it easy to identify with and relate to each other. We were both White, middle-class women attempting to effect change and improve the class climate with predominantly Black, low-income students.

Though Ms. Smith and I had similar cultural backgrounds, it was essential for me to use the Multicultural School-based Consultation framework, given that the students were culturally different, to determine if diversity might impact the case in any way. In order for me to understand the culture of the students, Ms. Smith and I openly talked about the impacts of race and socioeconomic status on her classroom. While it was intimidating at first to talk to Ms. Smith about cultural differences, it was an integral part of the success of the consultation process. Viewing her students through a multicultural lens allowed us to consider the broader implications of our work in her classroom. I also found it helpful that she was willing and open to talking about issues of diversity, especially in relation to issues that were occurring in her classroom, as well as in the school and the surrounding community.

I practiced attending and active listening during our meetings by keeping eye contact, nodding my head when appropriate, and translating and reflecting on what Ms. Smith said so that she knew I had heard her words correctly (Kampwirth & Powers, 2012). I also kept thorough notes while communicating with Ms. Smith. After our meetings, I reflected on what I had written in order to ask effective follow-up questions. I did this by probing more deeply when clarification was needed about a particular student or situation and by asking open-ended questions to follow up (Miranda, 2014). Examples of questions I asked included "What does bullying look like in your classroom?" and "What behaviors do you see as being the most problematic in your class?"

Although our communication was generally efficient throughout consultation, there were some skills I could have improved upon. Looking back, I could have been more assertive. I did not explicitly state what I wanted Ms. Smith to identify as the problem when we first started. She had trouble coming up with a behavior to target, and I was hesitant to give her a timeline for when the problem needed to be identified because I did not want her to feel rushed. I should have determined a goal date for problem identification so that we could have moved to the next step in the process more efficiently.

Problem-Solving Process

Problem Identification

In Ms. Miley's classroom, we identified the problem quickly and accurately. We identified the problem as relational aggression between the girls in her classroom. Relational aggression manifested in several behaviors, including gossip, put-downs, rumors, and social exclusion. We determined that the girls in Ms. Miley's class based their peer relationships on the identification with and desired membership in reputation-based peer groups. The rampant social comparison was problematic because it was leading to negative self-perceptions and relational aggression. In Ms. Miley's class, we noticed that girls used relational aggression to augment their own social statuses and also bring others' down. We hypothesized that this behavior had developed over many years and was influenced by their environments, including their communities, schools, and families.

We decided to focus specifically on the negative comments or put-downs between girls because these comments were clear markers of relational aggression. Ms. Miley collected baseline data during the times when her class was in her room. During this time, she made tally marks of the number of positive and negative comments she heard the students say. Though the problem was primarily with female students, the tally marks included comments from male and female students because this made it easier for Ms. Miley to collect data and captured the climate of the entire class. Using the baseline counts of positive and negative comments, we presented Ms. Miley with two interventions from which she could choose. In the plan implementation phase, Ms. Miley chose the intervention she preferred, Positive Peer Reporting (PPR), and began implementing it. We completed the final step in the problem-solving process—plan evaluation—by monitoring students' progress with data collection and by checking in to inquire about treatment integrity. This helped us to determine whether the intervention results could be attributed solely to a failed intervention or if a lack of treatment integrity contributed.

In contrast, the problem-solving process took more time in Ms. Smith's class. Ms. Smith initially had a difficult time deciding which behavior she wanted to target. After we had figured out which behavior was occurring most frequently, we were able to specifically identify and define the problem. As we were ready to gather baseline data, we then had to switch our direction. We originally planned to work with an individual student. After determining that working with that individual student was not going to work, we decided to tackle the problem Ms. Smith was facing with the girls in her classroom. This was when we realized that Ms. Miley was dealing with the same issue of female relational aggression. We also thought that teaming up would be beneficial for the teachers because they could assist each other in implementing the intervention. Our hope was that their collaboration would result in improved consistency for students, intervention procedural integrity, and teacher support.

We defined female relational aggression, and I (Mallen) observed her classroom in order to see the relational aggression happening in person and to determine if there were other factors contributing to the problem. After observing the students, I noticed that these negative interactions often seemed to arise unprovoked, where one student would put down another girl for no real reason. Other times, girls would begin to put each other down when they were placed in groups with students they did not like or who were outside their core group of friends. Once one girl made a comment, other students would occasionally begin to do the same. Other times, students would ignore the negative comment. Occasionally, the teacher would hear them and reprimand them.

For both teachers, we defined negative comments as put-downs or insults that generally centered on another student's appearance, academic performance, or family situation. We defined positive comments as praise, positive feedback, and compliments. After observing each classroom and hearing all of the negative comments that the fifth graders made, we decided to collect baseline data by counting the number of negative and positive comments said by students each day.

Next, we worked together to establish a clear goal for our intervention based on the baseline data. We asked both teachers to collect 4 days' worth of data to calculate their baseline scores. These 4 days' worth of data were averaged together to obtain the number of positive and negative comments and the baseline ratio for each class. After collecting baseline data, we determined that the students in Ms. Miley's class said an average of 0.25 positive comments and 5.75 negative comments each day (a ratio of 0.04). Ms. Smith's class said an average of 8.3 positive comments and 19 negative comments each day (a ratio of 0.44). We did not know the reason for the disparity between the two classrooms, but we suspected that it could have been caused by any of the following factors. First, although we defined the positive and negative comments the same way for each teacher, they may have interpreted the definitions differently. Second, since Ms. Miley and Ms. Smith each taught different subjects, the students in Ms. Smith's class may have had more opportunities to interact with each other. Third, Ms. Smith may have been more accepting of student conversation, whereas Ms. Miley may have been less tolerant of side conversations. This was evident in observations made throughout the duration of the intervention and the Girl Talk pullout group.

While Ms. Miley explicitly demanded the attention of her students by telling them that they needed to stop talking and listen, Ms. Smith talked over her students until she gained their attention. Though baseline data differed between classes, both teachers set the same goal for their classes. This goal was that the number of positive comments each day would be greater than the number of negative comments each day (a ratio of greater than 1.00). Though we guided the two teachers, they primarily determined the end goal for their classes, which empowered them to take ownership of the intervention.

In addition to completing a classroom-wide intervention, we wanted to further target the problem by focusing on the females in the fifth-grade class with a pullout group. We designed the curriculum for Girl Talk based on an existing program for young Black girls (Belgrave, 2008). We facilitated this 7-week program with the intent of increasing self-esteem and decreasing victimization and relational aggression. Throughout the entire process, we consulted with both teachers to design activities that would be engaging and educational for the students. Our goal was to teach the girls to replace negative put-downs with positive, appropriate interactions.

Intervention Design and Planning

We presented Ms. Miley and Ms. Smith with two interventions from which they could choose, Mystery Motivator and Positive Peer Reporting (PPR; Rathvon, 2008). Both teachers chose PPR. They thought that this would be more effective because it allowed students to learn and practice the skill of giving compliments. We believed that PPR would be effective in their classrooms because it was designed to enhance prosocial behavior and positive peer relationships. It also reduces negative or inappropriate behaviors by encouraging and reinforcing peer compliments (Rathvon, 2008). PPR fit well with our methods of data collection and our end goals for the two classrooms. We hoped that by encouraging compliments from students, we would see the number of negative comments decrease, which would ultimately reduce relational aggression in the classrooms.

Prior to explaining the specific steps of the intervention to the teachers, we gathered all of the supplies for them. This made it easy for the consultees to understand the protocol for the intervention and increased their chances of following through. The materials we chose were colorful and engaging for students, which we hoped would increase their interest in the intervention as well. Supplies for PPR included the honeypot (a glass fishbowl), colorful pom-poms to fill the honeypot, tally cards with each day of the week written on them for collecting progress monitoring data, and a set of instructions for the teachers to refer to if needed. After gathering the supplies, we taught Ms. Miley and Ms. Smith how to complete this intervention with their classes. In addition to completing the steps of the intervention, we instructed the teachers how to introduce the new activity to their classes. The teachers told their students that they were going to have an opportunity to help create a friendlier classroom atmosphere and to earn group rewards by participating in a new activity. They explained the basic process to their students and helped their students choose several rewards they could win. Finally, the teachers spent a few moments instructing students how to give effective compliments so they would know what to say during daily star sessions.

At the beginning of each day, the teachers chose two students from each class to be the stars for the day. Their names were written on the boards so other students could identify them. At the end of the day, the classes held star sessions where the other students in the classes complimented the stars based on what they had done well during the day. If compliments were vague or superficial, the teachers helped the students mold their remarks into effective compliments. The teachers recorded the number of compliments given that day. Each student who complimented the star was allowed to put one colorful pom-pom into the honeypot. When the pom-poms in the honeypot reached a reward level, the teachers were supposed to give their classes the rewards they had chosen ahead of time. Progress monitoring data were kept by recording tally marks of the total number of positive and negative comments made each day (the same way baseline data were collected). The teachers aimed to keep tally marks at least 3 days each week.

Intervention Implementation

Due to the fact that the intervention occurred over the course of the entire day, it was not possible for the consultants to monitor the intervention for treatment integrity in person. Instead, we relied on Ms. Miley's and Ms. Smith's reports of what was done and the data (tally marks and compliment recording) that were or were not given to us. Parts of this intervention were implemented consistently, while others were not. Ms. Miley consistently chose two students to be the stars and announced their names to the class. She also consistently held star sessions and kept tally marks. Ms. Smith was not as consistent at choosing the star students, as she said that her mornings were always hectic and that she occasionally forgot about the intervention. Ms. Smith consistently recorded the number of compliments said each day during the star sessions, but Ms. Miley was less consistent with recording the number of compliments each day. It was not fatal that the number of compliments during the star sessions were not consistently recorded because the tally marks were able to demonstrate if any changes in behavior occurred. Collecting data in two different ways (number of compliments and tally marks of positive and negative comments) helped to ensure that we were still able to measure potential change in the classroom.

Additionally, both teachers failed to complete the final step of the intervention: reward delivery. The lack of rewards the students received was a significant problem and may have played a role in the lack of change over the course of the intervention. When we set the initial reward levels on the honeypot, we told Ms. Miley and Ms. Smith that they could add an easier level if it seemed to be taking too long to reach the reward. We realize now that we should have been more specific in our instructions and that we should have followed up about the reward sooner. Two-and-a-half weeks into the intervention, the students still had not reached the first reward level. Ms. Miley reported at that time that she had not really seen a change in her students' behavior. Ms. Smith said that she was doubtful as to whether the reward would make much of a difference. If the students would have been rewarded within the first week, they may have been more motivated to continue to work toward larger rewards. However, even though the students chose the rewards they wanted (extra recess and a pizza party), they admitted that the rewards were insufficient to make them want to compliment their classmates. Therefore, it is also possible that the behavior still would not have changed with constant rewards. Based on the results of this consultation case, we are unable to determine if the intervention would work in the future with a similar class because the intervention integrity was compromised with the omission of a cru-cial step. As a consultant, it is essential that intervention integrity be maintained in order to have the highest chance of success. We learned that it is important to emphasize the importance of intervention integrity with consultees. If a con-sultant does not explain the importance of following consistent procedures, the consultees may alter the intervention, compromising the results.

Other than failing to reach a reward level, Ms. Miley and Ms. Smith perceived that carrying out the intervention was going well and they were not having any problems. We made sure to emphasize the importance of consistency with them during our consultation sessions so that the students recognized that compliments should be given every day. This was also important for the students in understand-ing that negative behaviors work against developing and sustaining a positive school climate (Goldstein & Brooks, 2007).

Evaluation

Both teachers monitored student progress by using tally marks to keep track of the total number of positive and negative comments made in their classes each day. In Ms. Miley's class, the 4 weeks of intervention data indicated that the aver-age number of positive comments was 0.90 per day and the number of negative comments was 8.10 per day (a ratio of 0.11). Though there were still many more negative than positive comments, the ratio did improve slightly from 0.04 at base-line to 0.11 during the intervention. It is doubtful that this represents a statistically significant change, however.

In Ms. Smith's class, the number of positive and negative comments fluctuated substantially throughout the 4 weeks that we kept data. The ratio of positive to negative comments during the intervention period was 0.57. When we would check in with her periodically, we noticed that some of the days were blank, with no tallies recorded for compliments on the tally card. We asked Ms. Smith about this, and she said that one of the days she had a substitute teacher and another day she had forgotten to pick the stars at the beginning of the day. She was very apologetic for missing those days. We reassured her that it was not detrimental to the results of the intervention, but the more data she collected, the more clearly we would be able to determine the effectiveness of the intervention. We also told her that if she forgot to pick the stars at the beginning of the day, she could still hold a star session at the end of the day where anyone could receive compliments. That way, students could continue to work toward their reward by compliment-ing their peers and adding pom-poms to the jar.

Though neither teacher saw changes in the comments their students made during the day, Ms. Miley noticed that the star students in her class would attempt to help their classmates throughout the day in order to be recognized. She believed that even though the data did not show behavioral changes, the intervention was valuable for the stars, since many of the students did not receive compliments on a regular basis. Unfortunately, our methods of data collection did not capture any changes in self-esteem that may have resulted from receiving compliments.

Closure

After 5 weeks of the classroom-wide intervention and 7 weeks of Girl Talk, we ended our time at Ackerman Elementary. The end date was primarily determined by the end of the academic year but was also informed by the lack of effective-ness of the intervention. During our final meeting, we discussed the successes and drawbacks of our intervention and pullout group. Both teachers indicated that they enjoyed both the intervention and Girl Talk even though we did not see any dramatic behavioral changes. They both believed that the entire process was ben-eficial because it helped their least confident students recognize their own positive attributes. Ms. Miley and Ms. Smith appreciated the collaborative framework of the consultation process and were willing to engage in consultation again in the future. After we finished working with the two teachers, we wrote and mailed a thank-you card to express our gratitude for their collaboration and support.

Though our intervention was not effective in producing significant changes in the climate of the fifth-grade classrooms, the consultation process itself was suc-cessful. Ms. Miley enjoyed the consultation process and viewed it as helpful to her classroom. Ms. Smith agreed that our efforts were not fruitless. We learned a lot about the consultation process and how we could improve in the future. The suc-cess of the consultation process was likely due to our perspectives on consultation; we truly believed that this was a collaborative relationship where the consultants and teachers contributed unique skills. We relied on the teachers to inform us as the experts of their classrooms and never assumed that we knew more about the classrooms than the teachers. We allowed them to decide which intervention would work best for their particular students, to participate in the design of the intervention data collection and Girl Talk curriculum, and to determine why the intervention or pullout group may not be working. In addition to valuing the expertise of our consultees, we were honest and realistic in the design of our interventions and data collection. Though our ideal design was for the teachers to collect intervention data every day, we realized that this would be cumbersome and overwhelming. We asked our consultees for their input, and they agreed that they could collect data three times per week. The consultation process was collaborative in the sense that we constantly asked for teacher input and allowed them to make decisions about the details of the process. More importantly, they willingly participated in sharing their ideas about what would work best. This ensured that they were committed and increased their follow-through, since their goals were self-chosen. Looking back on this consultation experience, we are certain that the process was smooth and beneficial to both the consultants and consultees because we valued the expertise of the consultees and ensured their investment by allowing them to make critical decisions about the intervention implementation.

Diversity Issues

Issues of diversity played a major role in this consultation case. Originally, Ms. Smith wanted to focus her intervention on an individual student who had a variety of both behavioral and academic concerns. It took Ms. Smith a while to decide which area she wanted to focus on first. By the time we had identified the problem, we were already a little over a week into our consultation, and we still had to get the permission slip signed from the student's mother in order to work with him on the intervention. Ms. Smith noted that she was unsure of whether the mother would actually sign the slip. There was a history of negative relations between Ms. Smith and this particular student's mother. Ms. Smith said that one of the reasons why his mother did not seem to like her is because she was a White teacher and the mother is Black. Ms. Smith commented that this student comes from a family that is involved in gang activity, and she is afraid that he is going to be the next involved. Because of the perceived cultural barrier between Ms. Smith and this student's mother, we had to redirect our intervention plan. The problem with this student's parent could also inadvertently explain why Ms. Smith made a few comments throughout consultation stating that this student behaves more appropriately with Black teachers than with her. This statement made us realize that Ms. Smith may be questioning her own effectiveness in working with her Black students, who comprised 95% of her classroom. We were concerned about this, because if teachers lose hope in their students, how much are the students actually going to learn? It could become a self-fulfilling prophecy for Ms. Smith in that she might not reach out to her Black students if she does not believe that she can effectively teach them. It is important to note that we cannot say with complete certainty that Ms. Smith's perceptions of her race and the race of her students made a difference in her classroom. While we noted a difference between her room and Ms. Miley's, there may have been other factors impacting their classes that we did not realize. Although Ms. Smith's perceived cultural differences were a barrier for moving forward with one particular student, it eventually allowed us to work together with both teachers and the fifth-grade class as a whole.

In comparison, Ms. Miley related to her students in a culturally appropriate way and was clearly confident in her ability to relate to her students. This could be because she is Black and used culturally relevant teaching strategies to connect with her students. It is important to note that the differences between the two teachers are subtle but are reflected in each teacher's belief in her own effectiveness in the classroom (as mentioned previously). One of Ms. Miley's greatest strengths is her ability to be a warm demander in her classroom. Warm demanders have extremely high expectations for their students; they constantly push them to succeed beyond what the students believe is possible. Additionally, they genuinely care about their students and express their care through these high standards (Delpit, 2012). Ms. Miley was knowledgeable about the students' backgrounds and sensitive to their needs. Despite racial differences (both consultants are White), we found it easy to relate to Ms. Miley. We recognized her cultural teaching style as one of her biggest strengths and as an essential source of information to aid our understanding of the problem of female relational aggression in her classroom.

Another issue of diversity involved the classroom-wide intervention. Students in both classes did not fully buy into the idea of the intervention. The intervention rewarded students for giving compliments to their peers as a way of targeting relational aggression. Ms. Smith noted that students would rather not say anything at all than give a compliment to another student because giving a compliment may be looked at as a sign of weakness. She also said that her students were not used to giving compliments and sometimes made negative comments to make themselves feel better. Ms. Miley agreed that maintaining status and dignity was more important for her students than earning a reward and showing weakness by complimenting someone they might not like. Both teachers' comments on this aspect of the students' behaviors were based on their years of working with minority, low-income students. In observing this behavior over the years, Ms. Smith and Ms. Miley have tried to understand its basis in order to facilitate change. While we were not familiar with the extent of this type of behavior, we were dependent on understanding it from both teachers.

Additionally, we realized early on in the course of Girl Talk that the way we were used to interacting with students was not culturally effective for the fifth-grade classes. Therefore, we observed Ms. Miley and modeled parts of our interactions with her class off of her teaching style in order to improve our classroom management. Brown (2004) found that the majority of urban teachers develop caring relationships with their students, establish business-like environments, demonstrate assertiveness, and clearly state and enforce expectations. Expressing assertiveness was especially important in this case. We began facilitating the group by simply hoping that the children would pay attention. Eventually, we realized that we must demand attention in order to receive it. One simple strategy Ms. Miley used was talking loudly but not yelling. Increasing the volume at which we addressed the group greatly improved their responsiveness. We also focused on improving our abilities to clearly state and enforce expectations, something Ms. Miley did well. While we initially phrased commands in the form of questions, we began to realize that this way of questioning was ineffective in an urban classroom. We began to use direct statements and followed up with the students to ensure compliance, which improved the flow and organization of the group.

It appeared to us that self-preservation was at the heart of the problem of relational aggression in Ms. Miley's and Ms. Smith's classrooms. Some of the most common put-downs both teachers noted were insults about another girl's physical appearance and insults about her family. From the teachers' perspective and observations, it seemed that for children at Ackerman, these two markers separated the lower middle class from the poor and the poor from the very poor. The higher income students likely had stable home lives and came to school dressed in clean, brand-name clothes. In contrast, the very poor students likely had unstable home lives and came to school dressed in unkempt, off-brand clothes. These students may have had to wear the same outfits to school multiple days in a row because it was their only option. Therefore, girls began to put each other down because, in doing so, it took the attention off themselves and showed the entire class that there was someone weaker, someone poorer, than them. Even as fifth graders, the girls in both classes were able to articulate parts of this. When asked why girls put each other down, they quickly indicated that they often do it to feel better about themselves. Once some of the students in the class began putting their classmates down, the others joined in in an effort to preserve their own dignity. They felt as if their only option was to put others down or be put down themselves. Pointing out others' flaws helped them maintain their self-esteem in spite of difficult situations outside of school.

This information was essential to the consultation process because it helped us understand why these behaviors were occurring. It also showed us that changing the culture of the classroom would be extremely difficult and might require more than an intervention and a girls' group. Furthermore, exploring the roots of relational aggression helped us determine how to tailor our interventions to the specific population. Interventions that work well with suburban White children may not work the same way with low-income Black children. Thus, it is essential to find evidence-based interventions or modify those interventions, taking into account the specific culture of the students in the class.

After learning about the population and climate of the fifth-grade classrooms, we began to question whether we, as White women, could connect with the girls during Girl Talk in a way that was culturally relevant. We used

Ms. Miley as a sounding board to help us design activities for Girl Talk that the students would enjoy and understand. We also spent one of our sessions talking about leadership. During this session, we brought in Black female guest speakers to serve as mentors and to inspire the girls. The guest speakers included four exemplary students from a neighboring high school, a graduate student in school psychology, and a professor of school psychology. Ackerman's principal (who is also a Black woman) made an appearance as well. Though we were somewhat limited in our abilities to culturally connect with the students, collaborating with classroom experts (like Ms. Miley) and similar role models helped us reach the students in a way that we could not have done on our own. In this way, consultation is truly a collaborative process where each member of the team contributes unique and invaluable expertise.

Lessons Learned

We learned that the best way to become skilled consultants is to work with real teachers and students. Although we are still developing our consultation skills, we learned a lot by practicing in the field on our own. Practicing in an urban elementary school exposed us to situations that we will encounter in future practice. First and foremost, we learned that building relationships is the most important aspect of consultation. The strong relationships we built with our consultees made the process flow smoothly, even when we were not sure what the next step should be. Had we not taken the time to build rapport with our consultees, they likely would not have agreed to our plans or followed through with their responsibilities. Building relationships with our consultees showed them that we were professionals who truly cared about their success.

Second, we learned the importance of explicit communication in consultation. In the intervention stage of consultation, we realized that the students had not been rewarded for their compliments, so we told the teachers that they could move the star lines on the honeypots that indicated reward benchmarks so that the students could receive the reward sooner. However, we did not specifically state how long they should wait before changing these benchmarks or how much they should lower the lines once they decided to do so. Because of our vague instructions, the teachers never moved their star lines to reward students. If we would have told the teachers explicitly how to change their reward benchmarks, the outcomes of the intervention may have been different. Teachers must fulfill many duties, so it is important to make the consultation process as straightforward as possible by clearly stating expectations.

Third, we learned that students need almost immediate reinforcement if we want to see a change in behavior. Otherwise, students have no motivation for changing. In this consultation case, part of the reason we believe that no real changes occurred was that students were never rewarded for their positive behaviors. Though the star students were motivated by the compliments they would receive at the end of the day, the rest of class was not motivated to give compliments because they still had not received the reward after 4 weeks. Had the teachers delivered the reward during the first few days of the intervention, the students may have gained some behavioral momentum through which they may have continued to increase their positive interactions with one another.

Fourth, we learned how to begin looking at consultation through a cultural context (Ingraham, 2000). Not only is it important to have an intervention that is culturally relevant, but consultants must also take into consideration the importance of working with teachers who are cultural mediators. Cultural mediators provide open discussion and interpersonal sharing with others about their own culture (Lynch & Hanson, 1998). Teachers such as the two in this consultation case can help novice consultants understand and appreciate cultures that may not be familiar to them. While Ms. Smith questioned her own effectiveness in working with her Black students, Ms. Miley was able to truly connect with her students, possibly because she herself was Black and understood the cultural context of her students. She was also better able to openly talk about the issues that the fifth-grade class presented, which dealt greatly with the diversity that was addressed earlier in the chapter. As two White consultants, it was advantageous for us to work with a cultural mediator like Ms. Miley so that we understood the students through a cultural context and were therefore better able to build positive relationships with them.

Finally, the most important lesson we learned from this process is that there are some classroom problems that are so deeply rooted that one intervention will not solve them. We anticipated this when we began the consultation process, which is why we also began Girl Talk. We had hoped that, through Girl Talk, we could begin to target some of the issues at the core of the relational aggression in the classroom. We believe that we did not see changes in students' behavior because the negative relationships that had developed over time served a purpose for the girls that we did not fully understand. In order to fully understand the function of their behavior, we would need to examine their home lives, community factors, and the school trajectory. Unfortunately, this in-depth ecological examination was outside the scope of consultee-centered consultation, so we attempted to make the best possible decisions with the limited information we had.

Additionally, the timing and relevance of the intervention itself influence the extent to which consultants can help change a classroom problem. We began our intervention in the middle of the school year around spring break, so we were battling months (and possibly years) of aggressive habits. We believe that our interventions could have been effective, but they probably needed to be instituted much earlier in the school year. They may have also been more effective if they were implemented with younger students, who are more likely to buy into the rewards system associated with the intervention.

If we were to face the same classroom problem in the future, we would begin the intervention and/or Girl Talk at the beginning of the school year. This would establish a communal, familial atmosphere in the classroom where students want to support one another. From the beginning of the year, students would learn that their classrooms are supportive places where positive behavior is rewarded. Ullucci (2009) discusses the importance for urban classrooms to focus first on building communities and teaching the students that their classes are also their families. Since building relationships is especially important in Black communities, starting the year with this intervention may have set a communal, familial tone for Ms. Smith's and Ms. Miley's classes. Students would have learned that it is important to treat their peers with respect because their peers are also their families. In hindsight, we should have also paid closer attention to Ms. Smith's classroom management style. While she expressed that being White may have been a barrier for her, it should be noted that she had 20-plus years in this school with this population. As novice consultants, it was difficult to determine if this was used as an excuse for why classroom management was more lax or if she really believed this. In the future, from an ecological perspective, more attention should be paid to how her classroom management style may have contributed to or exacerbated the issues occurring in her classroom.

In the future, we would begin building relationship skills at a younger age when peer influence is weaker and students are more malleable to change. Embedding social skills into all elementary classrooms could prevent later relational aggression. By teaching these skills earlier, we could prevent problems from developing rather than combating them once they emerge. From an early age, students would learn to value their peers and would feel safe in their positive, supportive classrooms. Additionally, helping teachers become aware of these aspects in their classrooms would assist them in managing their students more effectively, which would further promote positive change.

Questions for Reflection

- How can a consultant elicit change in a classroom where students or teachers come from a vastly different cultural background?
- How can a teacher's perspective of the diversity in his or her classroom affect his or her teaching style?
- In what ways can teachers help low-income students buy into the idea of a rewarding intervention?

References

Belgrave, F.Z. (2008). *Sisters of Nia: A cultural enrichment program to empower African American girls*. Champaign, IL: Research Press.

Bradshaw, C.P., Sawyer, A.L., & O'Brennan, L.M. (2007). Bullying and peer victimization at school: Perceptual differences between students and school staff. *School Psychology Review, 36*, 361–382.

Brown, D.F. (2004). Urban teachers' professed classroom management strategies: Reflections of culturally responsive teaching. *Urban Education, 39,* 266–289.

Civil Rights Data Collection. (2011). School characteristics and membership [Data file]. Retrieved January 24, 2015, from http://ocrdata.ed.gov/Page?t=s&eid=219092&syk=6&pid=732

Delpit, L. (2012). *"Multiplication is for white people": Raising expectations for other people's children.* New York, NY: New Press.

Goldstein, S., & Brooks, R.B. (2007). *Understanding and managing children's classroom behavior: Creating sustainable, resilient classrooms* (2nd ed.). Hoboken, NJ: Wiley & Sons.

Ingraham, C. L. (2000). Consultation through a multicultural lens: Multicultural and cross-cultural consultation in schools. *School Psychology Review, 29,* 320–343.

Kampwirth, T.J., & Powers, K.M. (2012). *Collaborative consultation in the schools: Effective practices for students with learning and behavior problems.* Upper Saddle River, NJ: Pearson.

Lynch, E.W., & Hanson, M.J. (1998). *Developing cross-cultural competence* (2nd ed.). Baltimore, MD: Brookes Publishing.

Miranda, A. (2014). Problem solving teams [PowerPoint slides]. Retrieved January 24, 2015, from https://carmen.osu.edu/

Rathvon, N. (2008). *Effective school interventions: Evidence-based strategies for improving student outcomes.* New York: Guilford Press.

Ullucci, K. (2009). "This has to be family": Humanizing classroom management in urban schools. *Journal of Classroom Interaction, 44,* 13–28.

Weinstein, C.S., Tomlinson-Clarke, S., & Curran, M. (2004). Toward a conception of culturally responsive classroom management. *Journal of Teacher Education, 55,* 25–38.

8

IDENTIFYING, UNDERSTANDING, AND NAVIGATING THE UNALTERABLES IN A CONSULTATION CASE TO EFFECT CHANGE

Nicole M. Brown

Advance Organizer Questions

- What types of verbal, nonverbal, self-reflective, and interpersonal skills should or must a novice consultant possess when entering consultation for the first time?
- Why is it important to become knowledgeable of a school's culture, climate, demographics, and any other administrative or structural elements prior to the consultation process?

School Culture and Climate

Central Magnet Traditional Elementary School offered a unique environment for my first experience as a novice consultant in the schools, one that taught me invaluable skills that I continue to use today. Central also shed light on a new concept for me: alterable versus unalterable factors. Alterables are the factors in one's life that are flexible and can be changed, also known as proximal variables. In contrast, unalterables, or distal variables, are the factors in one's life that cannot be changed and thus should not be dwelled upon when attempting to effect change (Howell & Nolet, 2000). There were some unalterables in this case that may have had an impact on the overall success of my intervention and, as I reflect on my experience, they taught me that I should instead focus on the factors that are within my power to change (i.e., the alterables). However, it is important to recognize and understand the unalterables in a consultation case because they are ever present. A few of the unalterables in this consultation case relate to the school and the changes within the school. At the time of my consulting experience, Central was undergoing administrative changes and building restorations that appeared to affect the climate of the school and may have impacted my consultation case. First, Central is a magnet school, which means that students from any of the surrounding regions can apply to go to Central and be entered into a lottery for enrollment. Central also focuses on a "traditional" approach in its learning mission, where the classrooms are mainly teacher directed and there is uniformity across students and grades (e.g., requiring students to wear red, white, and blue uniforms). Moreover, while awaiting renovation completion at its former location, Central occupied a swing space in a quaint, historic part of a large Midwestern city that can be described as a middle- to upper-class neighborhood. It should be noted that both the original school being renovated and the swing space were in the same neighborhood. Academically, the school has a rating of continuous improvement and consists of kindergarten through fifth grade. According to the state's education report card, the average daily enrollment is 296 students, 82% of whom are African American; 10% of whom are White, non-Hispanic; and almost 7% of whom are Multiracial. The school is considered high poverty; 78% of the students are economically disadvantaged, 58% are eligible for free lunch, and 8% are eligible for reduced lunch. Ironically, the population of the school does not reflect the population of the neighborhood in which it resides. Finally, there are 14 teachers at Central, almost 70% of whom have at least a master's degree, and a fairly new principal who assumed the principalship mid-year 2 years ago.

When considering the overall success of a school and its ability to prepare students for the future, it is not only important to consider the demographics of a school and the school setting but also its culture and climate. A school's culture and climate are imperative to the overall functioning of the staff and students. The climate of a school is simply the collective personality of its staff members, and it is greatly influenced by the individual teachers' perception of the school, their work within the classroom, and the informal and formal organizations of the school. The climate greatly impacts the behaviors of the school's staff because it is what sets schools apart from each other. The culture of a school is the belief systems, values, and structure that underlie its purpose and overall mission. Although these terms are vastly different, they both affect the overall functioning of a school (Hoy, 1990). Furthermore, it has been found that effective schools have strong cultures if they incorporate a set of particular elements in the school setting.

According to Hoy (1990), an effective school culture requires shared values and a consensus on how things should get done, and this must be established in order to build a strong school culture and an effective learning environment. This was seen at Central in the sense that those involved in the consultation process were eager to find a solution to the presenting problem and had the students' best interests in mind. From what I observed, student success and overall well-being were a core mission of most of the staff at Central, as there appeared to be a positive relationship between students and staff during morning routines, out at recess, and during dismissal. The second element—the principal as the hero or heroine who embodies core values—was harder to decipher at Central. Because the principal, Mrs. Peterson, was so new and because she was thrown into her position rather abruptly, it is understandable that there would be some resistance and dissension from the more veteran teachers. Furthermore, that the employees are also seen as situational heroes or heroines was seen less at Central due to a myriad of issues surrounding the school as they underwent numerous, sometimes stressful, changes. The teacher morale was low, and I witnessed a few interactions between teachers in which they discussed their lack of appreciation at the school or low feelings of worth that may contribute to another element: lack of autonomy and control. The remaining elements—rituals of acculturation and cultural renewal, rituals to celebrate and transform core values, and the connection between innovations and tradition—were not witnessed simply because of lack of opportunity; however, this does not mean that they were not being exercised. The presence, or lack thereof, of each of these elements really lends to the fact that culture and climate have a major impact not only on the staff relationships and perceptions but also on the students as well.

Multicultural School Consultation

Multicultural school consultation (MSC) is an adapted version of the traditional consultation process wherein the consultant adjusts the services in order to meet the cultural needs of the consultee, client, or both (Ingraham, 2000). Because culture is believed to influence the thoughts, expectations, and behaviors of the consultation process, it is absolutely paramount that the consultant consider these influences and attempt to embody the five components of the MSC framework. Additionally, the consultant is to "explore individual differences, as well as cultural issues, to prevent overgeneralization about cultural underpinnings at play, and to remain cognizant that culture is far more complex than the color of one's skin or the language one speaks" (Ingraham, 2000, p. 326). I found having a diversity class prior to my consultation class enormously beneficial, as I was able to practice these skills, examine my own biases, and self-reflect on my own MSC framework prior to and during the consultation process.

Relationships

I was a first-year doctoral student embarking on my first consultation case. This case involved two teachers and a 5-year-old African American male kindergartner. Due to the child being transferred to another classroom in the middle of the consultation process, I consulted with two teachers. The relationship between the consultees, Mrs. Teller and Mrs. Bowen, and myself, the consultant, was very positive. When considering the MSC component of cultural variations in the consultation constellation, or the similarities or differences between the consultant and consultee, the first consultee, Mrs. Teller, demographically resembled me as a Caucasian female in her mid to late 20s. Although Mrs. Teller had only been teaching at Central for less than 2 years, she was eager to work with me, and each interaction was always friendly and optimistic. She was always willing to help, and she was very determined to make the intervention a success. Mrs. Bowen, an African American female teacher in her late 30s, had been teaching at Central for over 15 years. Mrs. Bowen and I got along well, and she seemed genuinely interested in helping the student, even though she had not initiated the consultation process. The two kindergarten teachers appeared to be fine with the classroom switch, but both expressed their acknowledgement of their vastly different teaching styles. It should be noted that both failed to communicate with one another regarding the student's situation. As I gained more experience in my role, I later realized that it was very unusual for two teachers of the same grade not to collaborate, thus creating a potential barrier to the success of the behavioral intervention.

Communication Skills

In addition to fully engulfing oneself in the MSC framework, Safran (1991) outlined the importance of collaboration among the consultee and consultant, as well as the ability to exhibit proper communication skills, in order to have an effective consultation process in the school setting. First, the knowledge base is extremely important for both parties. This was definitely established, as both teachers had observed the behavior in multiple settings and had been in constant communication with the student's mother. From there, they were able to inform me of the situation so as to assist in building my knowledge base. Fortunately, both teachers had engaged in consultation before and therefore were willing to work with me by coming prepared to our meetings with relevant information.

Second, being skilled in interpersonal communication is crucial for consultants. This includes verbal and nonverbal gestures (e.g., eye contact, voice volume, etc.), good listening skills (e.g., ability to paraphrase, nodding your head, summarizing, etc.), expressing empathy, building rapport, and many more (Safran, 1991). Being a first-time consultant, my skills in communication definitely progressed as time went on. Although interpersonal skills were easily established between both teachers, other communicative skills, such as posture, paraphrasing, and speaking clearly, were ones that needed more practice. I learned in my consultation class the basic premise of good collaboration, communication, and consultation skills; however, it truly takes hands-on practice in the real world to understand one's strengths and weaknesses. By taping each consultation session with the teachers, I was able to review my communication skills, use of nonverbals, and overall consultant effectiveness so as to improve for next time. I immediately became aware of my lack of paraphrasing, lack of encouragement, and excessive use of unnecessary verbals ("umm"), which prompted my own self-reflection and self-awareness for subsequent sessions.

Finally, Safran (1991) mirrors the MSC framework by discussing the importance of the culture of the school and a cultural commitment between the consultee and consultant. Understanding and becoming aware of one's attitude, background, morals, and biases are necessary for both parties to consider prior to the consultation process because they can have a major impact, whether overt or covert, on its level of success. Although diversity and culture were a factor in this case, they did not present a major problem between the consultees and myself. Fortunately, I was able to empathize with both teachers and felt that a trust level had been developed. I also felt confident that we could work together to meet the needs of the student.

Problem-Solving Process

The problem-solving process is absolutely critical to successful consultation and is the cornerstone of applying ecological theory and the MSC framework (Meyers, Meyers, & Grogg, 2004). I also found it helpful to have a model to follow when working on a consultation case because it gave me guidance and structure during the process.

Problem Identification

The first interview with Mrs. Teller provided a lot of information on the presenting problem and the current behavior intervention with the student. Jordan, a young African American male in kindergarten who was in special education for speech, had been displaying a lot of disruptive behaviors and defiance toward adults. This had resulted in Jordan being suspended six times thus far, as well as receiving numerous other types of punishments (e.g., sent to the principal's office, a call home, in-school suspension, etc.). Unfortunately, research shows that this type of solution to "problem behaviors" with African American males is not uncommon. There is currently an overrepresentation of African American males being classified in special education as emotionally disturbed or being given suspensions or expulsions in hopes that this will "fix" the problem (Oswald, Coutinho, Best, & Singh, 1999). Mrs. Teller chose Jordan for a behavioral intervention in hopes that his behaviors could be properly addressed early enough.

An examination of the current behavioral intervention showed moderate to low success. The plan involved having Mrs. Teller color in a smiley face and allowing Jordan a trip to the class treasure chest every time he behaved. Because Mrs. Teller "bought in" to this intervention, I decided that in order to help Jordan, we would need to tweak the current intervention by making it empirically sound as well as including a component on appropriate emotion regulation. However, after about 2 weeks of starting the consultation process, Jordan's mother wanted him transferred from Mrs. Teller's classroom after a major incident (i.e., he hit Mrs. Teller) to the other kindergarten classroom because of differences that she felt Mrs. Teller possessed in her teaching and punishment style compared to the other teacher, Mrs. Bowen. Moreover, Jordan's mother had had previous experiences with Mrs. Bowen because she had taught her older son in the past. Therefore, I began working with Mrs. Bowen, who was a little reluctant to engage in consultation but was still determined to remediate the problem.

Her approach to Jordan's situation was vastly different than Mrs. Teller's. She believed that Jordan needed to learn how to appropriately respond to the word *no* and that there should be no disruptions in her classroom; therefore, she redirected Jordan until he listened, whereas Mrs. Teller would just ignore him until he listened. There were clear differences in personality, discipline and teaching style, and overall classroom organization and management between the two teachers. Mrs. Teller's classroom was highly structured and generally organized, whereas Mrs. Bowen's classroom was somewhat chaotic and disorganized. Mrs. Teller possessed a more nurturing personality, whereas Mrs. Bowen possessed a more authoritarian personality, both of which transcended into their respective teaching styles.

After meeting with Mrs. Teller and Mrs. Bowen and conducting a classroom observation, we were able to specifically identify Jordan's problems in school. Jordan had a hard time keeping to himself (e.g., not keeping his hands to himself, messing with other students' belongings, etc.) and not being in his assigned space (e.g., in his assigned seat or where he was supposed to be at the time of the day, whether it was on the mat, sitting in his seat, standing in a group, etc.). There were numerous incidents reported in a given week where Jordan would bother another student and refused to stay in his assigned space. When redirected in either instance, Jordan became defiant by yelling "No!", becoming physical (e.g., hit another student, kicked a teacher, scratched a teacher), or running out of the classroom. Oftentimes, these incidents resulted in Jordan being suspended, sent to the principal's office, or having to spend the day in the in-school suspension program.

Both teachers presented a case in which it seemed as if Jordan did not know his own boundaries and did not know how to respond when being told what to do in the classroom setting. Both teachers' narratives and each interaction I had with Jordan confirmed that he was a sweet and funny young boy; however, he was severely struggling with how to appropriately handle his emotions in situations in which he felt out of control. Because he was so young and because the incidents were so serious, significantly impacting his learning, it was imperative that these issues be addressed as soon as possible. After receiving information from Mrs. Bowen and Jordan's mother regarding his home life and after observing his behavior in school myself, we hypothesized several reasons for the behavior, including a mismatch between home and school expectations, classroom structure and environment, and Jordan struggling to modify his behavior to fit the expectations of the classroom environment. While the focus was on Jordan, the very different classroom management styles also needed to be considered. In both cases, neither teacher considered that the classroom environment might contribute to Jordan's behavioral difficulties. In addition, the behavior persisted in both classrooms despite very different classroom management styles.

Gathering baseline data of Jordan's behavior aimed to discover how often the problem behaviors occurred and, possibly, when and why. Baseline data were gathered as follows: For 3 days, Mrs. Bowen monitored Jordan's problem behaviors (termed *off-task behavior*) by focusing on two specific types of Jordan's problem behaviors (i.e., not keeping to himself and not being in his assigned space) so as to implement an intervention aimed at alleviating those specific problems. Mrs. Bowen was instructed to monitor the behavior in her own classroom during the same time each day. Mrs. Bowen was supplied with a Triple Tell Timer that was placed in her pocket and was preset to vibrate every 5 minutes (interval recording). For an entire hour each day, Mrs. Bowen was instructed to look at Jordan when she felt the timer go off in her pocket and decide whether he was on task (e.g., not exhibiting any of the problem behaviors) or off task (e.g., exhibiting one or more of the predetermined problem behaviors). If he was off task, she would make a tally on her clipboard. After the hour was complete, Mrs. Bowen added up the tallies and transferred them to a chart.

After Mrs. Bowen successfully gathered baseline data for 3 days, results showed that the off-task or problem behaviors occurred twice on the first day, not at all on the second day, and three times on the third day. Observations were recorded over the course of 2 weeks (Jordan was absent a couple days, and school was canceled one day, so the baseline data collection had to occur over a 2-week period). There did not seem to be a consistent occurrence of the problem behaviors nor a consistent antecedent to the problem behaviors; however, lack of control in a situation seemed to be an issue (e.g., the computer freezes up or shuts off while Jordan is working on it). Based on these results, the goal was to modify the current intervention and develop a new component to the intervention that would gradually decrease Jordan's problem behaviors and replace them with more appropriate behaviors (e.g., staying his seat, listening to the teacher's directions, not getting frustrated at something he cannot control). The terminal goal was to eliminate his problem behaviors completely.

Intervention Planning

Based on the information gathered from Mrs. Teller and Mrs. Bowen, observing Jordan in both classroom settings, and reviewing the results of the baseline data, the idea of the behavioral intervention plan was to give Jordan the choice to behave appropriately and to provide him with the necessary skills to help him become successful. It was indicated that Jordan works better in situations (whether positive or negative) where he feels that he is in control or has a choice. More often than not, his outbursts, whether verbal, emotional, or physical, were results of situations that were mostly uncontrollable to Jordan or situations in which he did not know how to react appropriately. Because it was hypothesized that he may lack skills that he was never given the chance to learn and practice, the intervention aimed to teach Jordan better ways of responding appropriately with his emotions, controlling his behavior, helping him self-monitor his behavior, and hopefully providing him with incentives that would help him become motivated to want to change his behavior.

Therefore, the intervention design for Jordan involved an emotion expression component, a self-monitoring component, and a Mystery Motivator component. The first component, emotion expression, simply involved the consultant meeting with Jordan during a free period in school and discussing with him instances when he feels upset or frustrated and more positive ways he could handle those emotions. By giving Jordan a small packet of faces that showed different ways to express one's emotions and teaching him what each one can look like in the classroom, Jordan could refer to it when he was not sure how he was feeling or how to react. The small packet gave him alternative ways to express his frustration (e.g., instead of throwing a chair because the computer froze, raise your hand and tell your teacher, take deep breaths when you start to get angry, etc.). The idea was to provide Jordan with some of the skills he lacked and help him realize that the way he reacted was getting him in trouble and that everyone was there to support him in actively trying to change these reactions.

The second component, self-monitoring, was an adaptation of the current behavior plan in place for Jordan. Because Jordan was already aware of the smiley face system and because he had had many discussions with his teachers explaining that he knows his behavior is getting him in trouble, it was fairly simple transitioning Jordan to the new behavior plan. Therefore, instead of having Mrs. Bowen color in a smiley face each time Jordan behaved, the smiley face sheet was taped to his desk every day so he could choose for himself after each period whether or not he should color the smiley face in. If he believed that he behaved that period, then he would color in the face; if not, then he would leave it blank. Of course, Mrs. Bowen was there to verify this self-monitoring, and if Jordan did not complete the task appropriately she would have to correct him. At the end of each day, if Jordan had five out of seven smiley faces colored in, he would get a sticker. After he received two stickers, he would then get the Mystery Motivator portion of the behavior plan.

The last component, the Mystery Motivator, is an intervention that delivers random rewards for desired behaviors. It consisted of five envelopes, each with a different incentive (e.g., spend lunch with the consultant, have the consultant read a book to Jordan during recess, get a prize, etc.) and some with no incentive but an encouraging note (i.e., "No reward today but maybe tomorrow! Keep up the good work!"). Jordan was prompted to then choose an envelope and receive the incentive the next day since the envelope choosing occurred at the end of a school day. The Mystery Motivator component was implemented because of its effectiveness, its use of performance feedback (i.e., receiving feedback based on his performance), and an intermittent reinforcement schedule (i.e., not knowing when exactly he would receive the reward motivated him to work harder in order to open more envelopes). This uncertainty of reinforcement, or a reward, has been shown in research to be extremely effective with students (Moore, Waguespack, Wickstrom, Witt, & Gaydos, 1994; Rathvon, 2008). Not only is it effective, but it is also easy to implement; therefore, it was the third component of Jordan's intervention plan. Throughout the entire intervention, positive support was encouraged to help Jordan choose more positive behaviors.

Implementation

The behavioral intervention for Jordan was implemented during the spring of the school year. Day 1 involved meeting with Jordan and teaching him about his emotion expressions and the intervention itself. Once understanding was established, I gave Mrs. Bowen the okay to start the intervention. The rest of the week and the following week were simply used as a treatment integrity measure. The intervention was implemented over a 12-week span; however, it was not implemented every day and rarely occurred on a consistent basis (e.g., 5 consecutive days) for a variety of reasons (e.g., spring break, suspensions, sickness, etc.). Therefore, I made sure to ensure integrity and compliance when the intervention was implemented by checking in and observing Mrs. Bowen use the three components each week. Because of the inconsistent schedule and because of reasons that will be discussed next, it was difficult to produce a data chart to show any success of the intervention.

Evaluation

The evaluation to ensure progress was established by meeting with Mrs. Bowen and observing the classroom each week. In addition, continued communication through phone calls and texting occurred between Mrs. Bowen and myself to keep each other informed. Over the course of 12 weeks, there were only two instances when I went to the school to deliver Jordan's reward (i.e., there were only two instances when he met the criteria of the intervention). Both times he opened an envelope, he received a reward, and each time was a play date with me during his recess, which we both truly enjoyed. Unfortunately, there were numerous occasions during the intervention that Jordan was suspended, taken out of school, sick, or on spring break that caused the intervention plan to be delayed.

As a result, the intervention rarely occurred consistently for at least 5 consecutive days in a week. These delays or interruptions in the intervention left me frustrated. As a novice consultant, I was unable to predict these inconsistencies and their subsequent effect on the success of our intervention. Due to the lack of consistency in implementation and reward delivery, the intervention did not prove to be successful.

Closure

Toward the end of the intervention, Mrs. Bowen felt defeated and basically gave up. I could sense her motivation depleting as the weeks went on. I kept trying to encourage her and keep her enthusiastic about the intervention, but as spring break approached and tensions between her and the principal increased, she began to complain to me more about her teaching situation than about the progress with Jordan. Data and charts began to diminish, and my hope for success quickly dissipated. Although there were a few instances of success and good behavior, overall, Jordan continued to display problem behaviors and did not seem to "buy in" to the intervention. We continued our efforts until the end of the school year, but because there were so many gaps within the intervention, I quickly realized that other factors, some factors that I could not control, needed attention in order to achieve any sort of success. For one, it was a deterrent that I was not officially part of the school staff. Coming in as an outsider or external consultant and trying to learn all the complexities within a school can be trying, especially during a rocky school year with so many administrative and building challenges. I was not sure if my being there was more of a help or hindrance to Mrs. Bowen once she officially gave up. Second, I continually wondered if Mrs. Bowen's classroom management style might actually be a contributing factor to Jordan's issues. Looking back, instead of adopting a defeatist attitude in this situation, I should have been more willing to look at the bigger picture and help Mrs. Bowen implement a more inclusive classroom environment, one that aims to teach more social and emotional skills that students may be lacking.

Diversity Issues

One of the challenges of diversity is making sure not to stereotype, or overreach, and make assumptions based on research about different groups. Thus, an ecological perspective is imperative in identifying the many alterable and unalterable factors and the potential barriers for success specific to your consultation case. Additionally, it is important to understand the various systems (e.g., family, school, personality) in one's life that interact and mediate one's psychological self (Bronfenbrenner, 1986). First, Central is predominantly African American and is considered high poverty with a label of continuous improvement in terms of academic standing. Central is a racially homogenous school (almost 90% of minority student demographics), with almost 80% of its students considered economically disadvantaged and almost 70% eligible for free and reduced lunch. Moreover, with a teaching staff that is predominantly White, it is important that the teachers are culturally competent when working with their students, something that is not often taught in teacher education programs (Kumashiro, 2012). Second, Jordan is an African American male kindergartener in special education for speech who lives with his mother and two brothers. Jordan's mother is a young African American woman who was very outspoken about Jordan's situation. Jordan's mother did not think that Mrs. Teller was the right teacher for Jordan, did not agree with Mrs. Teller's teaching style, and did not think that Jordan was to blame for his behavior; thus, she demanded that he be moved into the other kindergarten classroom after the New Year. While I am not sure that her perspective was valid, the principal chose to comply with the parent's wishes. One reason for the switch could have been because Mrs. Bowen had been teaching at Central for a longer period of time and/or because she had Jordan's older brother as a student in the past. While I did not pursue it, I later wondered if Jordan's mother felt more comfortable or hopeful that Mrs. Bowen would be able to provide the "right" discipline because she was African American and was familiar with the family. One issue regarding this barrier that I should have addressed, but did not realize until later, was the lack of communication between the teachers regarding Jordan's situation. The classroom switch and lack of communication between the teachers presented a potential barrier to the success of the intervention because had they been able to communicate, differences in classroom and teaching styles could have been discussed in terms of Jordan's needs instead of a trial-and-error run on which classroom worked better or worse for Jordan. In addition, while the school professed to have a behavior system, the use of suspensions appeared to be the main way of dealing with his behavior, even though majority of the infractions did not seem to rise to the need for suspension, especially for a kindergartner (with the exception of hitting others). Relying on suspension to deter unwanted behavior was concerning, as this is a common method of punishment for African American boys that has been shown to lead to dire consequences down the road.

Another potential barrier and possible issue of diversity appeared to be the vastly different environments Jordan lived in. His home life appeared to be unstructured based on information given by his mother, as well as the fact that his mother stated numerous times to the teachers that she did not think Jordan was doing anything wrong. Based on the mother's description of what happens in the home and the teachers expressing what they had seen or heard, it did not appear that there were consistent rules or consequences for misbehavior. This lack of structure collided with the amount of structure expected at a public school like Central, which uses a traditional approach in its teaching method. Although the switch to Mrs. Bowen's classroom more closely resembled his home environment of being less structured and more disorganized, the difficulty for him may have been compounded by the lack of classroom management by the teacher. While it could be hypothesized that Jordan's lack of structure at home contributed to his behavior and thus carried over into school, I had no way of verifying that this was actually correct. It is clear that each system of Jordan's life impacted his behavior, thus proving that interventions are required on more than one systems level in order to make a substantial change in his life.

There were some unalterables that may have also had an impact on this case. These include the structure of discipline in the home, a new principal in the school, and the relocation of the school. There are also other unalterables that I have come to realize occur in the school environment, such as the classroom, teachers, and demographics of student body. For example, as I spent more time in the building, through conversation with teachers, it became clear that the population of the school had changed over time. As little as 10 years ago, this was one of the most desirable schools in the district. It had a stronger middle-class base and was more racially and ethnically diverse. The school enjoyed an effective rating from the State Department of Education. Over time, the middle-class base has exited from the school, and it has become increasingly composed of lower income and minority students. When teachers commented on some of the academic and behavioral challenges in the school, they would often reference the population change in the school, almost as if what they do in the classroom does not matter. I found this a bit discouraging.

Because I am one who strives for immediate and positive change as a result of my work, this realization of unalterables was difficult for me to swallow. I could see the disconnect in Jordan's life, for example, and wanted to provide consistency and structure to his daily routine so that he could be given ample opportunity to learn and practice the skills that he seemed to be lacking. Although a stark reality, it is not entirely defeatist. We can make a difference and effect change if we understand and realize what factors are within our power to change. With that knowledge, an MSC mind-set, and the necessary skills, we can truly make a difference if we remain persistent, hopeful, and determined.

Lessons Learned

From an ecological perspective, there were multiple factors that could have contributed to Jordan's problem behaviors. In this instance, the teachers and I chose to focus on the individual child. Simply giving him a book full of emotions and briefly explaining to him how to express those emotions were not enough. In retrospect, Mrs. Bowen's classroom management should have been the focus of the intervention because it can be considered an alterable factor. The disorganization and sense of chaos that I observed suggested that she did not have a consistent classroom management system. For example, it took an unreasonable amount of time to transition from one activity to the next, and she often had to stop the activity or lecture because she did not have all of her materials handy. Too often, students are viewed as having a problem when a teacher's poor classroom management may actually be contributing to the child's problem. Mrs. Bowen's teaching style may not have been as effective for Jordan because he did not respond well to authority forcefulness and persistence. While Mrs. Bowen and I believed that it was important to teach Jordan that what he was doing was wrong, he also needed to be taught other skills to replace his problem behavior with more appropriate behavior. Jensen (2009) provides action steps for teachers to use in the classroom that help students learn and practice appropriate skills and behavior. For example, *embody respect* by giving the student the benefit of the doubt and not expecting all students to enter school with the same skill set, modeling appropriate behavior and allowing room for error, and disciplining students through positive relationships (e.g., pairing students based on peer modeling), not by exerting power and negative directives. Also, *embed social skills* in the instruction to enable students' learning of social and emotional skills by teaching basic social and emotional skills at the beginning of the year, allowing for collaboration among students, and implementing a social–emotional skill-building programs from evidence-based research models. Finally, *be inclusive* so as to create a welcoming environment where all children feel as if they are cared for and given ample opportunity to thrive. This last step involves praising students for appropriate behavior and celebrating effort as much as achievement; using inclusive language, such as "our classroom"; and acknowledging students' backgrounds and upbringings.

Unfortunately, due to inconsistent data collection, I could not say with accuracy that Jordan actually lacked skills that were necessary for success in the classroom. As a novice consultant, I think that it was easy to go down the road of seeing the problem as residing with Jordan rather than challenging the teacher on her classroom management style. While superficially addressed in the ecological model (examining multiple reasons for the problem occurring), I think that my lack of experience led me to go with the easiest solution, the problem residing with the child. Although I considered the ecological approach and tried to see the main systems impacting Jordan's life, I believe that I was also influenced by both teachers viewing the problem as Jordan's rather than truly examining the issue from multiple, sometimes obvious, perspectives (i.e., classroom management).

Moreover, I also underestimated how the change in school location and a fairly new principal of a seasoned staff could have an effect on Mrs. Bowen's morale. Some days she was in a bad mood because of a discussion she had had with the principal and was therefore reluctant to engage in the consultation process. As a result, our consultation sessions strayed at times from work-related issues to Mrs. Bowen's personal issues with respect to the principal. This situation definitely taught me how outside factors can play a major role in how consultees approach their jobs, similar to how students can have a bad day at home or in school and how that can greatly impact their behavior. Further, there was some disconnect between how Jordan should be punished at school. Mrs. Bowen firmly believed in suspension, but the principal was weary of that punishment due to Jordan's special needs classification in speech and his mother's involvement. Research shows that this type of consequence (e.g., suspension) is not likely to change the inappropriate behavior of the student and unfortunately may have more dire consequences down the road such as poor academic progress and student dropout (American Psychological Association Zero Tolerance Task Force, 2008). It was clear that there were differences of opinion in terms of best practice in assisting children with behavior problems. As I reflect on this particular issue, it would seem that the best approach in the future would be to address this as a schoolwide issue and work to move the school toward a positive behavior intervention support (PBIS) model. This would help reduce the reliance on out-of-school punishments, which tend to occur at a higher rate in urban schools, and potentially improve classroom management.

Finally, because a Mystery Motivator was used, it was clear that Jordan may have been motivated to receive the reward, but impulsive behavior and inability to control his frustration took over due to what appeared to be self-regulation issues. Thus, a more appropriate method could have been used that focuses on ability and skill deficits rather than treating performance and motivation (Moore et al., 1994). Also, the delivery of the incentive had to be the next school day because they were more social rewards and therefore the immediacy of the reward may have had an effect. Finally, as mentioned, the inconsistency of the intervention due to spring break, sick days, suspensions, and other factors definitely had a major impact on the overall success of the plan. Although frustrating at times, it was a good lesson on the realities of working in schools versus a clinical-type setting.

In summary, there were many factors involved in this case that truly demonstrate the importance of an ecological perspective in understanding a child's overall functioning in the context of home and school and how diversity may play a role in the consultation process. It is absolutely necessary for a novice consultant to not only approach any consultation with an MSC framework in mind but to also be aware of, and confident in, one's ability to make a difference in any way possible. In this case and cases like it, adopting the MSC mind-set ensures that you will examine all evidence of diversity because that allows you to truly open up your mind, ears, and eyes to the reality of the situation. It is not enough to be aware of the diversity- and cultural-related issues that loom within and outside of schools; you must be self-reflective and self-examining. You must be aware of your own biases so that you do not find yourself in the trenches of stereotyping. This includes being aware of the diversity research but carefully examining whether it applies to the individual student with whom you are working. This experience truly taught me the benefits of an MSC framework, the ecological perspective, the potential barriers to consultation due to diversity, and what I as a novice consultant can do to effect change in a student's life.

Questions for Reflection

- How can you determine whether the culture of a home environment or the core family beliefs of a client collide with those of the school's learning mission? What can you do if that conflict exists and negatively impacts the client's learning?
- How can adopting the MSC framework aid in understanding the "bigger picture" and thus aid in your ability to make a difference in the client and/or consultee's life?
- When does it become clear that certain unalterables in a client's life are out of your control, and what can you do to effect change with that realization?
- Why is the issue of diversity one of grave importance when engaging in a consultation relationship? How does this relate to the barriers of consultation success?

References

American Psychological Association Zero Tolerance Task Force. (2008). Are zero tolerance policies effective in the schools? An evidentiary review and recommendations. *American Psychologist, 63*, 852–862.

Bronfenbrenner, U. (1986). Ecology of the family as a context for human development: Research perspectives. *Developmental Psychology, 22*, 723–742.

Howell, K.W., & Nolet, V. (2000). *Curriculum-based evaluation* (3rd ed.). Belmont, CA: Wadsworth Cengage Learning.

Hoy, W.K. (1990). Organizational climate and culture: A conceptual analysis of the school workplace. *Journal of Educational and Psychological Consultation, 1*, 149–168.

Ingraham, C.L. (2000). Consultation through a multicultural lens: Multicultural and cross-cultural consultation in schools. *School Psychology Review, 29*, 320–343.

Jensen, E. (2009). *Teaching with poverty in mind: What being poor does to kids' brains and what schools can do about it.* Alexandria, VA: Association for Supervision and Curriculum Development.

Kumashiro, K.K. (2012). *Bad teacher: How blaming teachers distorts the bigger picture.* New York, NY: Teachers College Press.

Meyers, J., Meyers, A.B., & Grogg, K. (2004). Prevention through consultation: A model to guide future developments in the field of school psychology. *Journal of Educational and Psychological Consultation, 15*, 257–276.

Moore, L.A., Waguespack, A. M., Wickstrom, K.F., Witt, J.C., & Gaydos, G.R. (1994). Mystery Motivator: An effective and time efficient intervention. *School Psychology Review, 23*, 106–118.

Oswald, D. P., Coutinho, M. J., Best, A. M., & Singh, N.N. (1999). Representation in special education: The influence of school-related economic and demographic variables. *Journal of Special Education, 32*, 194–206.

Rathvon, N. (2008). *Effective school interventions: Evidence-based strategies for improving student outcomes* (2nd ed.). New York, NY: Guilford Press.

Safran, J.S. (1991). Communication in collaboration/consultation: Effective practices in schools. *Journal of Educational and Psychological Consultation, 2*, 371–386.

PART IV
Culturally Competent Consultation Practice Leads to Success

9

THE CULTURALLY CONFIDENT CONSULTEE

Successful Multicultural School Consultation

Carly Tindall

Advance Organizer Questions

- What factors contribute to successful consultee-centered school consultation?
- How can teacher attitudes and beliefs affect intervention outcomes?
- In what ways do factors such as school culture and climate impact consultee-centered consultation relationships?

ABC Elementary School Culture and Climate

School culture and climate are important factors for consideration when engaging in school consultation. Culture and climate permeate beyond the physical walls of the classroom, affecting relationships among the consultant, consultee, and client. When engaging in consultation from a multicultural school framework, considering the culture and climate of the school system is essential in order for the consultant to be able to gain a more holistic understanding of the consultant–consultee relationship. As a novice consultant, I spent time the first couple of weeks interviewing Ms. C and observing her classroom in order to assess the impact of school culture and climate on ABC Elementary School. From numerous interviews and observations, I learned that ABC Elementary School provided academic services to a population of economically disadvantaged students (95.3%). Ms. C stated that many of her students' families had constrained social mobility and had experienced generations of economic disadvantage. ABC Elementary was located in an urban neighborhood plagued with high occurrences of gang activity. Students expressed gang affiliations, and issues pertaining to these associations infiltrated beyond the community into the classrooms. The large majority (95.1%) of students at ABC Elementary were racial minorities and lived within a few blocks of the school. In contrast, the large majority of teachers at ABC Elementary were White and lived outside of the community in which the school was located. Third grade reading guarantee data indicated that proficiency levels in reading and math were 43.8% and 35.4%, respectively. The state's Department of Education designated the school to be in academic emergency according to performance and achievement standards. Halfway through the case study, ABC Elementary School began a reconstitution process due to consistently insufficient academic achievement and improvement. As a stipulation of this process, all teacher contracts were terminated for the following year with the possibility of only 50% of teachers being eligible for rehire.

Relationship of the Consultant and Consultee

The case at ABC Elementary School involved consultant–consultee ethnic similarity and cross-cultural classroom–consultee and classroom–consultant relationships. Myself, the consultant, and Ms. C, the consultee, identify as White females. The classroom was 88.5% African American, 6.6% Caucasian, and 4.8% Multiracial. Ms. C described her students as a diverse group of individuals with many struggles outside the classroom. Ms. C was an enthusiastic, energetic teacher in her mid to late 30s. Ms. C had 13 years of teaching experience as a third-grade teacher, 11 of which had been spent at ABC Elementary School. Ms. C was considered a mentor teacher at ABC Elementary School and would observe struggling teachers and provide feedback and strategies for building their classroom management and teaching skills. Ms. C volunteered to engage in a case study conducted by a school psychology program student involving cross-cultural consultee-centered consultation. Ms. C was open to engaging in the consultation process and saw it as potentially beneficial in helping with some problem behaviors in her classroom. I was a 23-year-old first-year education specialist student participating in my first consultee-centered case consultation.

Communication Skills

Ms. C was enthusiastic and excited about engaging in the consultation process. She was welcoming toward any constructive feedback regarding the presenting problem. In our initial interview, Ms. C stated that as a mentor teacher in the school, she often observed other teachers and provided constructive feedback. Being the only mentor teacher at ABC Elementary, Ms. C did not have the opportunity herself to engage in constructive feedback regarding issues specific to her classroom. Therefore, Ms. C sought out opportunities to receive feedback to build upon her skills. This foundation for the consultation process and relationship created opportunity for effective communication and interpersonal skills, assisted in building rapport, and ultimately contributed to the success of the intervention and consultation process. The communication skills utilized through this process included attending, active and reflective listening, empathy, and questioning (Kampwirth & Powers, 2012). During conversations and interviews with Ms. C, I demonstrated the importance of the consultee's opinion and communicated my interest in her thoughts by maintaining eye contact and using appropriate facial mannerisms. Active listening is an important communication skill, as it provides the consultant with an understanding of the content and emotional content of the message being communicated. By reflecting back keywords spoken by Ms. C, I was able to gain a clear understanding of the issues Ms. C was experiencing. Making empathetic statements to Ms. C allowed me to establish referent power during the consultation process. Ms. C believed that I valued the same things as her and therefore respected my role in the consultation process. I asked questions to gain insight into the issues experienced by Ms. C but to also assess her opinion and attitude about the issue and subsequent intervention (Kampwirth & Powers, 2012). I believe that I was able to establish and maintain an effective and successful consultant–consultee relationship through the implementation of these communication skills. While I believe that I demonstrated good communication skills during my first consultation experience, I am clearly aware that there is room for continual improvement. I believe that the consultee's style of communication assisted in my effective use of communication.

Presenting Problem

Ms. C volunteered for consultation due to her concerns regarding the classroom noise level during unstructured transitional periods, defined as transitions to recess, specials (e.g. music and physical education), lunch, and class dismissal. Ms. C was primarily concerned about the transition to the coat closet just prior to the end-of-day dismissal. Ms. C specifically stated two areas of concern related to her classroom: (a) the noise level during the unstructured transition to the coat closet and (b) off-task behavior, defined as talking, physical contact with peers, and students being out of their seats during the unstructured transition to the coat closet. Ms. C provided me with specific information regarding the primary concerns listed previously. I conducted two classroom observations to gather information and record data concerning the decibel level and occurrences of off-task behavior during unstructured transitional periods to the coat closet at the conclusion of the school day. Information obtained through consultation sessions with Ms. C and baseline data gathered during observations of the classroom during unstructured transitions to the coat closet suggested that

Ms. C's perception of noisiness was greater than the actual noise level presented in the baseline data. On the basis of this information, I proceeded to develop an intervention to reduce the average noise level during unstructured transitional periods, specifically during the transition to the coat closet, and provided Ms. C with information regarding cross-cultural awareness and understanding of normative levels of noise.

Problem-Solving Process

Problem Identification: Baseline and Goal Discussion

Following numerous consultation sessions and classroom observations, Ms. C and I were able to collaboratively identify and define the problem concerning the noise level during unstructured transitional periods, specifically the transition to the coat closet at the end of each school day. When engaging in problem analysis, I asked the consultee about her interpretation of the problem. Ms. C stated that her students were excessively noisy during unstructured transitional periods such as recesses, specials (art class, physical education class, etc.), and transitioning to the coat closet. I observed Ms. C during multiple unstructured transitional periods, including morning arrival, the start of class, lunch, specials, and the transition to the coat closet. The purpose of these observations was twofold: (a) to gain information and collect data regarding the issue Ms. C had described in our consultation sessions and (b) to observe Ms. C and evaluate the ways in which she operated within the context of her classroom and her interaction with students. During observations, I was able to collect data related to the perceived problem of the noise level by recording the decibel levels using the smartphone application TooLoud? to establish baseline data. I provided Ms. C with a data collection sheet and demonstrated the method of gathering and recording baseline data. Ms. C was very excited about using the smartphone application and indicated that she believed that she would be able to collect and record data throughout the intervention. Through demonstrating how to collect baseline data, I provided Ms. C with the first record of baseline data. Ms. C collected the final two records of baseline data. Baseline data indicated that the average classroom decibel level during the transition to the coat closet at the end of each school day was 69.33 dB. After analyzing the baseline data, Ms. C and I discussed the results and concluded that Ms. C's perception of the noise level was supported by the data. During this consultation session, Ms. C and I defined the problem and established a goal for the intervention. Ms. C stated that she believed that a decibel level of 65 dB or below would be suitable during unstructured transitions to the coat closet. The goal for the intervention was defined as: "The classroom will maintain an average decibel level of 65 dB or below during unstructured transitions to the coat closet at the conclusion of each school day."

Intervention Design and Planning

Intervention design and planning involved identifying and establishing an appropriate intervention. A review of the data collected during classroom observations throughout the consultation process suggested an intermittent reinforcement intervention, more commonly known as a Mystery Motivator intervention (Moore, Waguespack, Wickstrom, Witt, & Gaydos, 1994). Mystery Motivator interventions utilize a random reward schedule to reinforce goal behaviors and can be utilized in both an individual and classroom-wide intervention. This specific case required a classroom-wide Mystery Motivator intervention. When I presented the implementation design to Ms. C, she stated, "I've tried that intervention in the past and it just doesn't work." Kampwirth and Powers (2012) identify this type of teacher as the "I did it, but it didn't work" teacher. I listened to Ms. C explain why she did not believe that the intervention design was suitable for her classroom. After listening to her opinions and reflecting back her concerns, I engaged Ms. C in a more comprehensive, step-by-step explanation of the design and the benefits of implementing intermittent reinforcement intervention designs. I explained that making rewards in contingency-based interventions unpredictable can significantly enhance the power of the contingency (Rathvon, 2008). After further explanation regarding the benefits of the intervention design, the consultee retracted her previous opinion about the intervention and stated, "This sounds like something my kids would love!" With support and understanding from Ms. C, the Mystery Motivator intervention was developed. Ms. C downloaded the smartphone application TooLoud? to her cell phone. I provided her with six charts, one for each week of the intervention, which were displayed on the whiteboard at the front of the classroom. This location was visible to all students. Each chart contained five squares that were covered by pieces of paper. "X"s were intermittently drawn on the chart in a random order but remained hidden under the pieces of paper. I provided Ms. C with envelopes, the amount of which equaled the number of "X"s present on the six charts, containing rewards for meeting the intervention goal. Rewards included pencils, erasers, stickers, and extra center time (i.e. time when students would get to participate in various activities' stations including computer work, coloring, reading, playing board games).

Table 9.1 is an example of the chart utilized by Ms. C to record data during baseline data collection and to record data throughout the implementation of the intermittent reinforcement intervention. The chart provided space to record the time, date, highest decibel level, average decibel level, and occurrences of off-task behavior, as well as a section for notes.

Intervention Implementation

Ms. C was effective and consistent in implementing the intervention and providing the appropriate reinforcement. She reliably and accurately implemented each

TABLE 9.1 Data Collection Table

DATE	TIME	HIGHEST RECORDED DECIBEL LEVEL	AVERAGE DECIBEL LEVEL RECORDED	OCCURRENCES OF OFF-TASK BEHAVIOR	NOTES

step of the intervention process and recorded the decibel level. Each day, the consultee would follow these instructions:

- Verbally state expectations regarding an appropriate noise level to students by saying, "We are working toward a noise level of 65 dB or less."
- Begin recording decibel level through the smartphone application TooLoud? on cell phone.
- Place cell phone with the application TooLoud? recording the decibel level on the projector so students can monitor the current decibel level being recorded.
- Dismiss students in groups to the coat closet.
- When students have finished in the coat closet, record the average decibel level.
- If decibel level is at 65 dB or below, remove a square on the Mystery Motivator chart and reveal if an "X" is present under the square.
- If an "X" is present, the students receive a reward:
  o Open an envelope to reveal the reward for the students.
  o Hand out the reward to the students.
- If an "X" is not present:
  o Verbally praise the students for meeting the goal and encourage them to try again the next day.
  o If the decibel level is above 65 dB, do not remove a square on the chart.
- Verbally instruct the classroom to try to meet the goal the next day.

To ensure integrity, I observed Ms. C implementing the intervention. During this observation, she followed the intervention script and executed each step of the intervention as instructed. The students were knowledgeable of the expectations and excited about the intervention. They achieved the goal by receiving an average decibel level of 60 dB, resulting in receiving a reward for maintaining adequate levels of noise during transitions. During the observation, both the students and Ms. C were excited about the Mystery Motivator intervention. Ms. C provided verbal praise, and students celebrated silently by fist pumping when they achieved average decibel levels below 65 dB.

Evaluation

The final step of the problem-solving process, plan evaluation, involved progress monitoring through recording noise-level data and evaluating the implementation of the intervention through integrity checks. By conducting an integrity check, I was able to ensure that Ms. C was implementing the intervention as instructed and thus that the noise-level data were valid. The data collected by Ms. C were analyzed, and results indicated that the intervention was successful (Kampwirth & Powers, 2012).

Figure 9.1 shows the average decibel level recorded during baseline data collection and the average decibel level recorded during the implementation of the intermittent reinforcement intervention. Three days of baseline data were collected, with average decibel levels at 70, 68, and 70 dB, respectively. Six days of data were collected during the intervention implementation, with average decibel levels at 60, 60, 42, 55, 50, and 48 dB, respectively.

Ms. C recorded the average decibel level for the first 6 days of the intervention. After these 6 days, she no longer recorded data but continued to implement the intervention with continued success. I accepted that Ms. C was no longer recording the decibel level because she continued to implement the intervention as I had explained and demonstrated. Furthermore, Ms. C was extremely

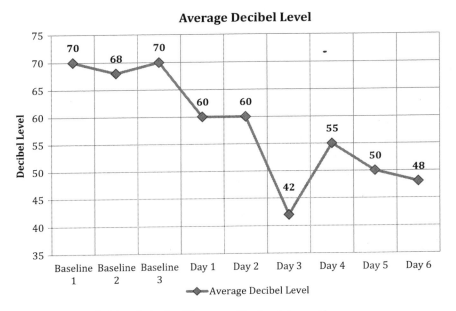

FIGURE 9.1 Decibel Levels in the Classroom During Intervention

pleased with the intervention. She discussed how she had begun using the smart-phone application during other classroom activities. The limited record keeping allowed for minimal data to assess progress monitoring of the intervention. The data received revealed that after the initial implementation of the intervention, the noise level during the transition to the coat closet did not exceed the goal of 65 dB. These data serve as evidence for the effectiveness of the Mystery Motivator intervention in reducing the noise level during transitional periods.

At the conclusion of the consultation process, I discussed the intervention with Ms. C to assess her opinions regarding implementation, usefulness, success, etc. She stated that when the students understood the expectation (65 dB or less) and could monitor themselves (viewing the smartphone application on the projector screen), they were much more likely to meet expectations.

Closure

The final consultation session between Ms. C and myself provided an opportunity to discuss the intervention and overall consultation experience. When the consultee and I discussed the Mystery Motivator intervention, she stated to me, "I will never stop using this [Mystery Motivator intervention]. The kids just love this. They're doing so awesome!" Ms. C informed me that she had begun using the smartphone application TooLoud? during multiple transitional periods through-out the day. The consultee reflected on her prior hesitation in implementing a Mystery Motivator intervention and stated that she had tried similar interventions before, but none had been quite as successful. It seemed that the success of this particular intervention had restored her trust and understanding in the efficacy of intermittent reinforcement interventions such as the Mystery Motivator intervention. She thanked me for my assistance during the consultation process. At the conclusion of the consultation experience, I felt as though Ms. C had benefited from the Mystery Motivator intervention and the consultation experience as a whole. I felt that my consultation skills, as a novice consultant, were valued within the consultee-centered consultation relationship.

Diversity Issues

The success of the intervention and consultation process is largely attributed to Ms. C's confidence, cultural competency, and respect for diversity. During observations, I discovered that Ms. C demonstrated self-confidence in her teaching and classroom management skills in her cross-cultural classroom (Ingraham, 2000). Ms. C understood her third-grade students and the challenges they faced. Weinstein, Tomlinson-Clarke, and Curran (2004) state that teachers can engage in effective classroom management through knowledge of their students' cultural backgrounds; understanding of the broader social, economic, and political context;

ability and willingness to use culturally appropriate management techniques; and commitment to building caring classrooms. Ms. C encompassed all of these characteristics into her classroom management and curriculum, which contributed to her effectiveness as a teacher. Through classroom observations, I was able to observe Ms. C inquiring about her students' lives outside of the classroom. During an observation during which students were arriving to school, Ms. C asked a student about a dentist appointment he had had the previous day. She asked another student about how her younger siblings were doing at home. She engaged multiple students in conversation regarding various aspects of their home lives. Ms. C was knowledgeable of the neighborhood in which her students lived. During our first interview, she provided me with information regarding the neighborhood where ABC Elementary was located. She talked about poverty rates, gang-related activity, and other neighborhood facts that impacted her students. These practices reflected Ms. C's knowledge of her students' cultural backgrounds and economic context of the neighborhood and communicated Ms. C's commitment to building caring classrooms.

Ms. C established and reinforced social norms in her classroom. Weiner (2003) states that these practices are important in urban education to allow trusting relationships between teachers and students. Ms. C was able to establish such trusting relationships with her students by explicitly stating socially acceptable expectations. Prior to beginning any classroom activity, Ms. C would state the expectation. As she saw students demonstrating stated expectations, she would verbally provide positive reinforcement by recognizing and praising students. For example, this case involved expectations regarding noise level. Prior to unstructured transitions, Ms. C would provide the class with expectations of the average decibel level. This practice of providing clear expectations allowed students to understand and demonstrate appropriate behavior in the classroom environment. By engaging in this practice, Ms. C communicated to her students that she respected them, and in turn Ms. C's students were respectful of her.

During consultation sessions when discussing the problem of noise level with me, Ms. C was critical in examining her own biases by stating, "Our principal says that we need to alter our expectations regarding noise level and the students in our classrooms. Maybe that is part of the problem. Maybe I need to change my expectations." This statement provides evidence of Ms. C's ability to examine her own cultural biases, which further demonstrates her cultural competency. The culmination of these factors contributed to not only the success of the intervention but also largely to Ms. C's success as a culturally competent teacher.

Lessons Learned

This case illustrates the importance of cultural competency in relation to successful consultation, intervention development and implementation, and classroom management. At the conclusion of the intervention, the classroom consistently achieved desired decibel levels of 65 dB or less during unstructured transitions to the coat closet. Ms. C was impressed and satisfied with the outcomes of the intervention. She provided valuable insight regarding consultation across cultural contexts. The results from this case study suggest that teacher confidence, attitude, and cultural competency are major contributors to student success in the classroom.

The multicultural school consultation (MSC) framework describes four domains in which consultee learning and development occur. One of these domains, confidence, is of important consideration in this case. The MSC framework states that some consultees experience diminished self-confidence in cross-cultural situations due to a lack of competency because of limited knowledge or skill with clients of minority cultural groups (Ingraham, 2000). This framework also states that consultees motivated by fear of failure, rejection, or the unknown may be challenged in cross-cultural exchanges (Ingraham, 2000). When examining this case through the MSC framework, several important similarities exist between the literature and the factors at ABC Elementary. Ms. C was teaching in a setting where the majority of her students were identified with a minority cultural group. In addition, ABC Elementary was dealing with a political process of reconstitution, which eliminated job security for all teachers. This process created a culture of fear, failure, and uncertainty within the school system. Ms. C demonstrated confidence despite these opportunities for diminished confidence. The confidence exhibited by Ms. C in this case supports the MSC framework, which states that consultees who are competent in MSC learning and development domains, including confidence, are successful in multicultural school consultation (Ingraham, 2000).

Ms. C engaged in a relational approach to classroom management, which increased her third-grade students' ability to establish trust in her (Gregory & Ripski, 2008). This relational approach, defined by Ms. C's empathic nature toward her students, assisted in the effectiveness of the intervention but also in her abilities to manage her classroom overall. Ms. C genuinely cared about the success of her students, and this factor allowed for successful results from the Mystery Motivator intervention. Ms. C was able to recognize her own cultural biases and how these biases contributed to the perceived problem of noise level during unstructured transitional periods. This practice of recognizing cultural biases contributed to Ms. C's affiliation as a culturally competent teacher. I appreciated Ms. C's willingness to address issues of diversity head on. As a result, we were able to explore how issues of diversity may or may not impact the case we were working on. I believe that this case increased my knowledge and skills in cross-cultural consultee-centered consultation.

Reflecting on the consultation process, I learned that consultee attitudes can greatly influence intervention outcomes. Research has validated the use of Mystery Motivator interventions, but the consultee's attitude in adopting the intervention largely determined and perpetuated its demonstrated success. From discussions with and observations of the consultee, I believe that the reliable implementation of the intervention could be attributed to her belief in the intervention itself. The consultee was confident in her abilities and skills in understanding and working with diverse students. This confidence contributed to the consultee's attitude of self-improvement. Because the consultee was confident in her skills, she was open to implementing new ideas, including the Mystery Motivator intervention. If the consultee had not believed in the intervention or had lacked confidence in her skills to effectively implement the intervention, she may not have implemented the intervention as reliably as demonstrated in this case. Her confident attitude and support toward the intervention contributed to positive intervention outcomes.

The combinations of characteristics demonstrated by the consultee, which I believe contributed to the success of this case, are of important consideration for future consultation sessions. The consultee in this case was eager to receive support and feedback regarding her skills in her multicultural classroom. She demonstrated cultural competency and respect for diversity in the ways she spoke of and to her students, the ways in which she interacted with her students, and the ways in which she committed herself to being knowledgeable about the community in which her students lived. The consultee adopted and implemented the Mystery Motivator intervention with integrity. These characteristics are certainly not unique to the consultee, but the combination of such cannot be an assumption for which all consultee competencies in consultation relationships are considered. In future consultation relationships, it will be important to evaluate and consider consultee attitudes and competencies in relation and in comparison to this case.

Questions for Reflection

- In what ways can consultation experiences with culturally competent consultees be utilized in working with consultees who may lack confidence?
- In what ways can consultees with less confidence than demonstrated in this case gain confidence?
- Can consultants influence consultee attitudes regarding multicultural school consultation? If so, in what ways?

References

Gregory, A., & Ripski, M. B. (2008). Adolescent trust in teachers: Implications for behavior in the high school classroom. *School Psychology Review, 37,* 337–353.

Ingraham, C. (2000). Consultation through a multicultural lens: Multicultural and cross-cultural consultation in schools. *School Psychology Review, 29,* 320–343.

Kampwirth, T.J., & Powers, K.M. (2012). *Collaborative consultation in the schools: Effective practices for students with learning and behavior problems.* Upper Saddle River, NJ: Pearson.

Moore, L.A., Waguespack, A. M., Wickstrom, K.F., Witt, J.C., & Gaydos, G.R. (1994). Mystery Motivator: An effective and time efficient intervention. *School Psychology Review, 23,* 106–118.

Rathvon, N. (2008). *Effective school interventions: Evidence-based strategies for improving student outcomes.* New York: Guilford Press.

Weiner, L. (2003). Why is classroom management so vexing to urban teachers? *Theory into Practice, 42,* 305–312.

Weinstein, C., Tomlinson-Clarke, S., & Curran, M. (2004). Toward a conception of culturally responsive classroom management. *Journal of Teacher Education, 55,* 25–38.

10

CULTURAL UNDERSTANDING AND COMMUNICATION

Keys to Successful Multicultural School Consultation

Abigail Baillie

Advance Organizer Questions

- What specific consultation skills are most salient for effective consultation in urban elementary schools?
- What is the role of the consultant's confidence in a successful consultation case?

School Culture

Woodland Elementary is a neighborhood elementary school within a large urban school district. A majority of the children who attend Woodland are African American students who face poverty. This elementary school is rated as one of the lowest performing schools within the state. Prior to the school's current principal, five principals have worked at Woodland over the past 7 years. Recently, Woodland underwent new staffing because of the school's state designation of academic emergency. Because of the new staffing and the school's urgency to make adequate yearly progress, Woodland's new principal is firm with academics and supportive of the staff. Additionally, she works hard to gain community support for her building and for the students who attend the school. She actively seeks grants and resources to better support the students within Woodland Elementary. The principal is connected with families within the building and communicates with these families to understand their needs. The new staff members who were brought on board have a passion for working with children in urban communities. According to Cuthrell, Stapleton, and Ledford (2010), having staff members who are invested in their students may be the most important determinant of success for children in urban schools. In addition to a supportive principal and invested teachers who make contributions to a positive school culture, the diverse population of students at Woodland bring their own culture into the school building.

When working with diverse populations, it is essential that teachers and other school staff members understand the school culture. This is particularly important when considering the students' success rates, the students' and teachers' motivations, and the teachers' willingness to implement new strategies. It is equally important that the teachers, staff, and consultants understand that their culture may be vastly different than those of the children and school (Kampwirth & Powers, 2012). It is through these characteristics of school teachers and other staff members that urban schools find success.

Classroom Culture

Within Ms. J.'s classroom, there was a firm, but caring, culture. She clearly conveyed her authority without acting harshly or unsettling her students. She was consistent in her expectations and provided support when students were not having the best day. She established relationships with her students and frequently reminded students that their success was dependent on their efforts. Her students knew the routine of the classroom and respected Ms. J.'s position within their class.

As mentioned previously, it is important that teachers understand that their culture may be very different from that of their students (Kampwirth & Powers, 2012). In Ms. J.'s classroom, she understood this concept clearly. Although Ms. J. is Caucasian and a majority of her students are African American, this did not pose a problem in her classroom. She made comments during the consultation process indicating that she knew of these differences and that, because of this, she needed to adapt her teaching strategies to better fit her students' needs. One of the clear attributes that helped lead to the success within Ms. J.'s classroom was the fact that she recognized her students' cultural differences and challenges but did not view them as an obstacle to her ability to teach effectively, nor for learning to take place effectively. For example, Ms. J. noted that some students may not have the ability to complete work at home or that some students did not know if they were going to have a meal available after school. Ms. J. did not allow these things to change her perspective on these students. She did not make negative comments about her students and their challenges, but instead expressed a sincere desire for her students to succeed.

Consultant–Consultee Relationship

At the beginning of the consultation process, Ms. J. seemed flustered with the idea of completing an intervention. She made several comments alluding to the fact that she was overwhelmed and that this consultation case was just another thing she had to juggle during her school day, despite the fact that she had volunteered to participate in the consultation process. To overcome this challenge, I began expressing empathy to Ms. J., letting her know that her job is difficult and she does have to juggle a lot. In addition to empathy, I reassured Ms. J. that this process was not going to be a challenge and that I would be there to provide her with all the help that I could offer. After several consultation sessions, we were able to overcome the slight resistance she showed at the start of the consultation process. Open-ended questions and friendly consultation meetings allowed Ms. J. and me to determine the classroom problem that she wanted to address. Throughout the consultation and intervention process, she was willing to give suggestions and try suggestions that I had proposed. We were able to discuss techniques that would work best in her classroom through frequent and productive communication. Finally, as the intervention process began, she was very diligent with data collection and excited to see results. Ms. J. noted that this process was easy and that she would definitely implement the intervention strategy in the future.

We built a relationship throughout this process that allowed us to work together collaboratively and effectively. This relationship was one of the most important factors that helped lead to the success of the intervention. Ms. J. began this process with a hesitant attitude toward the intervention process. However, through effective communication and support, Ms. J. experienced a perspective change that allowed the consultation and intervention processes to occur with little difficulty.

Communication Skills

Kampwirth and Powers (2012) noted that there are several communication skills that are essential to successful consultation. These skills include active listening, empathy, and effective questioning. Frequent and productive communication played a large role in the consultation process. Because of the fact that time was limited for meetings between myself and Ms. J., it was essential that we be able to communicate via other means. We e-mailed frequently, and if she had an immediate question regarding the intervention process, she contacted me via text message.

The time that we were able to meet in person was extremely valuable. During these brief meetings, I built rapport by expressing empathy and showing a genuine interest in her classroom. Similarly, I helped Ms. J. identify classroom problems through effective and open-ended questioning. We established goals through collaborative decision making. While discussing the problem, goals, and interventions with Ms. J., I often asked several open-ended questions to gain a clearer picture of her expectations for the class. Additionally, I found it imperative to check for understanding and clarification along the way to ensure that nothing was being missed in our discussions. Ms. J.'s ability to communicate was also a contributing factor to the success of the consultation process. She was clear when describing a topic and expressed willingness to consider different approaches. Finally, at the end of each meeting or e-mail communication, I found it very helpful to summarize the content we had just discussed. This allowed me to highlight the decisions we made and discuss our future plans for the intervention process. Reviewing the material ensured that no information was lost throughout the meeting and that future steps were clear.

Problem-Solving Process

Problem Identification: Baseline and Goal Discussion

The first step of the problem-solving process, as discussed by Kampwirth and Powers (2012), is problem identification. Initially, this step was a bit difficult for Ms. J. However, through empathy and rapport building, we overcame this challenge. At the beginning, Ms. J. identified two problems that were both classroom-wide behaviors. After discussing both problems in depth, we decided that we would target her classroom's negligence in turning in completed reading homework logs. In the future, Ms. J. hoped to increase her students' motivation to complete homework assignments in several subject areas. She wanted her two reading classes to independently complete their reading logs each night and bring them back to class the next day. After identifying the problem, we decided upon an observable and measurable definition to reduce confusion when determining if the student's reading log was complete. A completed reading log was defined as:

> All appropriate sections on the reading log are completed at the end of independent reading time. These sections include genre code, author, date, title, read alone/read with help/read to category, an adult's initials, and the child's rating of the book.

Once we had defined the problem in clear terms, Ms. J. collected baseline data for 5 days. We used baseline scores to examine the number of students who completed their reading logs before Ms. J. made any changes. At the end of independent reading time in both her morning and afternoon classes, Ms. J. tallied the number of students who had completed reading logs each day.

After we identified the problem and collected baseline data, Ms. J. and I discussed her goals. She had high expectations for her class because "[she] knew they could do it." Ms. J. noted that at the beginning of the intervention, she wanted at least 60% of her class to complete their reading logs daily. After reviewing the baseline data and explaining that the kids need to be successful in order to see an improvement in reading log turn-in, we decided at the beginning of the intervention that after the first week the goal would be for 25% of the students to turn in their reading logs. As the intervention continued, our goal increased so that by the middle of the intervention (the end of Week 2), we would see 50% of students turning in their reading logs. By the end of the intervention (Week 4), we would see at least 80% of students turning in their reading logs. We wrote our overall goal as follows: At least 80% of students will have a completed reading log at the end of independent reading time each day.

Problem Analysis

The second step in the problem-solving process, as described by Kampwirth and Powers (2012), is problem analysis. Here, we discussed the problem more in depth, including reasons why reading logs were not getting returned. Several of the reasons Ms. J. noted involved characteristics of the children's home or events that took place outside of school. After discussing these reasons, we decided that providing children with motivation in class was the best way to improve their behavior. We discussed the idea that providing the children with in-class motivation might help remind them to finish and return their completed reading logs. Initially, we used immediate and tangible rewards to motivate students. Over time, as the rewards became less frequent, the hope was that the students would begin to develop their own levels of motivation that were not entirely based on a tangible reward.

Intervention Development: Design, Planning, and Implementation

After identifying and analyzing the problem, the next step in this process was intervention development. First, before discussing possible interventions, I asked Ms. J. what she had tried in the past to increase the number of students who turned in their completed reading logs. She mentioned that she had previously tried several types of rewards, but they were often inconsistent and eventually faded out. She noted that her class would be motivated by a reward for a couple of days and shortly after lose interest. After hearing this, I suggested that a Mystery Motivator would be appropriate for her class because this intervention is consistent and involves a choice of rewards. Ms. J. was unfamiliar with this specific intervention but was eager to try it. Rathvon (2008) states that the Mystery Motivator intervention is appropriate to improve homework completion. Additionally, the author notes that "the Mystery Motivator intervention has been demonstrated to have powerful effects on homework completion and accuracy for elementary school students and is highly rated by both students and teachers" (Rathvon, 2008, p. 173).

After discussing the most appropriate intervention to use in Ms. J.'s classroom, I created an intervention script to ensure that the Mystery Motivator intervention was implemented with integrity each day. Ms. J. provided me with several rewards that the class had decided they would like to work toward. These rewards included candy, lunch with the teacher, computer time, 5 minutes of free time, a mechanical pencil, or a chance to be the student teacher of the day. I provided Ms. J. with all of the materials needed for the intervention. The materials included the Mystery Motivator chart, a chart to tally which students completed their homework logs each day, the intervention script, the reward menu, and the tangible rewards. I adapted the intervention script from Moore, Waguespack, Wickstrom, Witt, and Gaydon (1994). The script for Ms. J.'s classroom stated:

> At the start of the intervention, Ms. J. introduced the Mystery Motivator to the class. She explained that the students would have a chance to earn a reward if they completed their reading logs daily. She reviewed what a completed reading log consisted of, according to our definition mentioned previously. She posted the definition of a completed reading log and introduced the Mystery Motivator chart. Each card on the chart represented each day of the week. On the front of the cards the number of students that needed to have a completed reading log, to meet the expectation for that day, was written clearly. If the daily expectation was met, the students were instructed to flip over the card. If an X was revealed when the card was flipped, students received the voted-upon reward for that day. If the back of the card was blank, Ms. J. congratulated the students and reminded them that they had another opportunity to earn a reward the next day.

Ms. J. implemented the intervention in her classroom for a total of 4 weeks. After the fourth week, data were collected with no intervention being implemented. Ms. J. tallied the number of students who completed their reading log each day for the final week. We then examined these data to determine the overall effectiveness of the Mystery Motivator.

During the intervention implementation, I monitored treatment integrity through observation. I observed the intervention take place on two occasions: once in the morning class and once in the afternoon class. Based on my observations in the classroom, the intervention script was followed, as Ms. J. checked the reading logs, counted to see if the appropriate number of children had completed their reading logs, allowed the class to flip over the card, and provided verbal affirmation or a reward promptly following the card being flipped.

Evaluation

Each week, I collected the data sheet from Ms. J. where she had marked the amount of completed reading logs she had received per day. Data sheets consisted of class rosters and blank boxes to mark if each student's log had been completed for the day. Ms. J. was diligent in filling out the data sheets daily and having them completed when I came into the school. The data logs suggested that the intervention showed early positive effects. This was shown by the number of students who had completed the logs during baseline collection nearly doubling after the first week of the intervention. During the baseline phase, the average number of students who completed their reading logs daily was nine for Class A and eight for Class B. After the first week of the intervention, the average number of students who completed their reading logs each day jumped to 14 (Class A) and 12 (Class B). The number of children in both of Ms. J.'s reading classes who had completed their logs daily remained consistently high throughout the intervention process. We achieved positive results with this intervention because of the consistency in implementation and varied reward choices. Ms. J. stated that she really liked the intervention and was already thinking of new ways to use the Mystery Motivator to improve other classroom behaviors.

Closure

After 4 weeks of implementing the Mystery Motivator, Ms. J. and I briefly discussed the overall effectiveness of the intervention. The intervention was effective for both her morning and afternoon classes. As shown in Figure 10.1, the amount of reading logs completed increased consistently in both classes. In my final discussions with Ms. J., she noted how this intervention improved her students' motivation to complete their homework. Although the reward was not presented every day, the class participation in completing the reading logs remained high. Because the students did not know exactly which day they would receive a reward, they continuously worked to accomplish the goal and gain a prize.

In discussing the intervention's long-term effects, it was recognized that it is important to slowly lessen the amount of rewards provided. Ms. J.'s long-term goal was to increase the students' motivation to complete assignments. This was done by providing a tangible reward frequently throughout the beginning stages of the intervention and then slowly decreasing its frequency over time. She shared that she did have concerns that removing the physical reward would decrease participation. However, when one looks at the results, homework completion did not decrease significantly after the intervention was removed, and the results did not resemble the lack of homework completion that the baseline data present. This suggests that students may have increased their level of motivation to complete reading logs. After the final weeks of this intervention, Ms. J. indicated that she wanted to continue to use this intervention in her classroom to increase her class's homework turn-in rates.

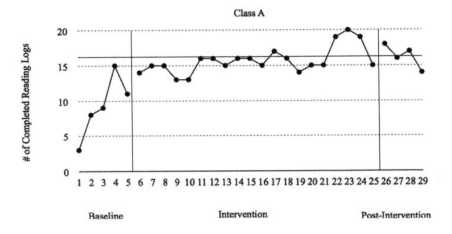

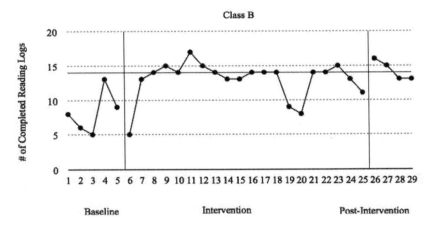

FIGURE 10.1 Reading Log Completion

Reasons for Success

When reflecting on this consultation case, there are several reasons why this intervention succeeded. Ms. J. possessed several components Ingraham (2000) discussed that are essential to multicultural school consultation (MSC). These include the classroom culture, Ms. J.'s understanding of her students and their needs, Ms. J.'s ability to communicate, high teacher acceptability of the intervention, and intervention integrity. In addition to Ms. J.'s contributions to the success of this intervention, providing materials to her also aided in the intervention's success. If Ms. J.

would have had to gather and create the intervention supplies on her own, she may have never had enough time to complete the intervention in an organized and efficient way. Each of these factors contributed to the overall success of this intervention in a specific way.

When thinking about consultation through a multicultural lens,

> educators who create culturally relevant learning contexts are those who see students' culture as an asset, not a detriment to their success. . . . Students are expected and empowered to develop intellectually and socially in order to build skills to make meaningful and transformative contributions to society.
> (*Milner, 2011, p. 69*)

This consultation case was successful because of Ms. J.'s presence in her classroom and her ability to understand her students. Within the domains of MSC, one must be able to understand one's own culture while respecting and valuing others' cultures (Ingraham, 2000). When one entered this classroom, Ms. J.'s expectations for her class were clear. She set her standards high and held students accountable for their work. Ms. J. ran her classroom in an authoritative manner where although she valued discipline, she also built relationships. Ms. J. frequently adapted her teaching style in order to best educate her students. This quality enabled Ms. J. to be successful when she implemented the Mystery Motivator. She was open to trying new techniques in her classroom that would help her students succeed.

Additionally, MSC involves individuals being able to communicate cross culturally. Ms. J. not only had the willingness to adapt her teaching practices to better fit her classes' needs, but she also communicated well with me throughout this entire process. This was beneficial, as it made the problem-solving steps easy to accomplish. She was able to explain to me the level of her students' performance, why their performance may have been at that level, and the level of expectation that she had for her students. Communication during this process helped to identify the specific problem in a more concise manner, develop goals and design the intervention, and ensure that the intervention was being carried out appropriately. Our frequent and clear communication was integral to the success of the consultation process.

Ms. J. exhibited cultural competence, classroom control, and excellent communication skills throughout this experience. A final contribution to this intervention's success was the fact that I provided all materials to Ms. J. This made the intervention simple. For Ms. J., there was no preparation needed, no materials to be collected, and no handout needing to be copied. Each week, I made sure that Ms. J. had all of the necessary materials needed and that all of her questions were answered. Additionally, I collected the data each week from the previous week. For this case, providing the materials helped to relieve some of Ms. J.'s stress and prevent her from feeling overwhelmed by the new procedures we implemented. This also helped Ms. J. carry out the intervention with integrity. Because I provided her with a script and materials, Ms. J. knew exactly what to do each day. There was nothing that she needed to create on her own. Having all of the components of the intervention prepared helped to ensure that the intervention was completed correctly. By letting Ms. J. know that this process was not going to be complicated and by aiding her along the way, the consultation case was successful.

Diversity Issues

During the consultation process, when identifying the classroom problem, Ms. J. noted several issues of diversity that may have been impacting her class. For example, Ms. J. noted the following: Some children did not have opportunities to complete the work outside of school because they are transient; it was difficult for them to bring assignments home and back to school; and in some of the children's homes, homework was not a priority. Here, Ms. J.'s concerns for the students may represent a difference of culture between herself and the students, meaning that Ms. J. has homework completion expectations that may not be the same as those of the students and families that Ms. J. works with. Ms. J. stressed the importance of schoolwork being done and completed in the home. However, this may not be possible for many families living in the neighborhood that Woodland Elementary occupies because there are other stressors that take a more prominent focus in their lives. For example, families in this neighborhood may be focused on getting things done to have their daily needs met (i.e., food, shelter, and clothing).

As summarized in Cuthrell, Stapleton, and Ledford (2010), previous research suggests that schools view the parents as having three primary roles regarding their children's education. First, parents serve as a resource in the education of their children. Second, parents are supporters of their children's education. Third, parents are participants in their children's education. In schools that have a disproportionate number of low-income populations, parents' views of their roles regarding their children's education may differ from the school's view. The parents' and school's view of parental involvement may differ due to cultural differences between the family and school staff, parents' attention focused on meeting other needs (i.e., food and clothes), or the school's lack of understanding of the challenges families in poverty face. This in no way means that they do not care about their child's education, because many of them do. Because of the lack of resources that they are able to obtain, their attention may be focused on meeting the needs of their families. These are important notions to consider when examining issues of homework completion, as each entity may view their roles differently. Although the view of homework may have differed between Ms. J. and some of her students, she did not allow this to impede her perceptions of these students in a negative way. Instead, she recognized this difference and attempted to find beneficial ways to bridge this gap in her classroom.

Lessons Learned

Throughout this consultation experience, I learned several important lessons. One of the most prominent lessons that I discovered is that the teachers with whom I work will look to me as an expert in my field even when I am still a novice consultant. Although I was a novice consultant, Ms. J. was willing to try anything that I suggested. She was receptive to my opinion, and we were able to consult with one another as colleagues, as opposed to a student and a professional. Although I am just learning these skills, it is important that I practice them with confidence. This lets teachers and other professionals know that I am aware of what I am supposed to be doing and that I am going to do my best to make sure that my skills are as proficient as possible.

Another lesson that I learned throughout this consultation process is that sometimes it is necessary to be persistent. Because I, as a student, was not Ms. J.'s first priority, there were times when I would have to ask her twice for information or provide her with reminders of meetings that we had scheduled. At first I was hesitant because I did not want to seem as though I was bothering her, but as time went on I learned that she valued my persistence. In some cases, she had simply forgotten about our meeting times or to return my e-mails, so she often thanked me for the reminders. Having persistence and not allowing problems or questions to linger will make for a more effective and efficient consultation process.

In hindsight, this experience was very beneficial, as I was able to work with a teacher who understood her students. Although Ms. J. had vastly different experiences from the majority of the students in her classroom, she was still able to create a learning environment that fostered academic success in her students. She was motivated to adapt her teaching practices to best fit her students' needs. Working with a teacher who truly understood the cultural differences between herself and her students allowed me to better understand the mechanisms that work best in MSC. Because I have worked with a teacher who is successful in teaching in a diverse classroom, I am better equipped to work with other teachers in my future practice. Through working with Ms. J., I gained insight into the way in which teachers can better understand students who may be culturally different from themselves. In future practice, I can use this insight to help other teachers better understand students in their classroom and practice effective MSC.

Overall, I enjoyed my consultation experience at Woodland Elementary. Ms. J. was exceptional to work with, as she was eager to try new strategies within her classroom. I learned a great deal about urban classrooms through my consultation meetings with Ms. J. and my observations in her classroom. This experience helped me to understand the ways in which confidence in your abilities, understanding the cultural context of the students in a classroom, and persistence are essential to the consultation process.

Questions for Reflection

- Communication skills between the consultant, consultee, and students played a large role in this consultation case. In what ways were the consultant's and consultee's communication skills most effective within this MSC example?
- In this case, the consultee understood the difference between her own culture and that of her students. How was this component of the MSC framework effectively used within the consultation process?

References

Cuthrell, K., Stapleton, J., & Ledford, C. (2010). Examining the culture of poverty: Promising practices. *Preventing School Failure, 54*, 104–110.

Ingraham, C. (2000). Consultation through a multicultural lens: Multicultural and cross-cultural consultation in schools. *School Psychology Review, 29*, 320–343.

Kampwirth, T.J., & Powers, K.M. (2012). *Collaborative consultation in the schools: Effective practices for students with learning and behavior problems.* Upper Saddle River, NJ: Pearson.

Milner, R.H. (2011). Culturally relevant pedagogy in a diverse urban classroom. *Urban Review, 43*, 66–89.

Moore, L. A., Waguespack, A. M., Wickstrom, K. F., Witt, J. C., & Gaydon, G. R. (1994). Mystery Motivator: An effective and time efficient intervention. *School Psychology Review, 23*, 106–117.

Ohio Department of Education. (2012). Ohio Avenue Elementary School: 2011–2012 school year report card. Retrieved February 15, 2015, from http://archive.education. ohio.gov/reportcardfiles/2011–2012/BUILD/028423.pdf

Rathvon, N. (2008). *Effective school interventions: Evidence-based strategies for improving student outcomes.* New York, NY: Guilford Press.

11

A TALE OF TWO TEACHERS

How Collaboration Sparks Success in Consultation

Kristen N. Heering

Advance Organizer Questions

- What strategies could a novice consultant implement when confronted with teacher resistance to attempt to strengthen and reinforce the collaborative aspect of the consultation process?
- What tools did Ms. Meredith employ in her classroom that Mrs. Experience did not? How did the use of these tools contribute to the success of a collaborative consultation relationship?

School Culture

My first two consultation experiences took place within the walls of Sunshine Traditional Elementary School, which is situated in a middle- to upper-middle-class area near downtown in a large Midwestern city. The school serves approximately 290 students in Grades K–5. The school is unique in that its enrollment is lottery based, so the majority of students who attend do not reside in the neighborhood in which the school is located. According to the school's 2011–2012 school year state report card, 84.5% of the students enrolled are Black, non-Hispanic; 7.2% are White, non-Hispanic; and 6.9% are Multiracial. About 78.3% of the students enrolled are considered economically disadvantaged, which predicates the school's current high poverty status overall. The school was designated as a continuous improvement school by the State Department of Education for the 2011–2012 school year, and the school achieved adequate yearly progress.

The school has a long-standing practice of having a "traditional" approach which, according to its current foundational beliefs, consists of structured routines and a well-disciplined environment. With its Eagle mascot; red, white, and blue uniforms; and daily recitation of the Pledge of Allegiance, the school also seems to have a patriotic theme. Over the years, the school has experienced population shifts and a reduced focus on the school's theme of "tradition." Thus, in some ways, what used to be tradition has been lost. Through discussion with the school's fairly new principal, she herself stated that many of the teachers espoused different definitions of what tradition means for the school. It seems that there may be a disconnect between what the mission and vision are with what is actually occurring in the school. The principal also shared that she views frequent occurrences of insubordination as problematic and as something she would like to see change. In keeping with the tradition theme, there was an expectation that there would be respect for authority from the students in the school. Both teachers and the principal view this as having been compromised in the past several years. On several observations, I did indeed witness at least two instances of insubordinate behavior. It seems to me that the staff and administration may well need to explore why this type of behavior is increasing. As Greene (2008) states, most challenging kids already know the expectations we hold for their behavior, but they are lacking important thinking skills needed to self-regulate their behavior.

Related to this overarching issue of insubordination in the school are the school's discipline policies. Within the first classroom in which I was working, a student who threw a pencil at a peer was subsequently suspended for this behavior. When this occurred, the student was verbally scolded and told immediately to leave the room; no subsequent discussion took place to try to understand the student's behavior or to provide the student with corrective feedback about the behavior. While this was only one instance I observed, there appears to be a critical missed opportunity to utilize situations where students exhibit unexpected behaviors to engage in thoughtful reflection of the behavior that occurred and why it occurred. In addition, school staff could possibly use these situations as teaching tools for students so that they are more equipped with the skills needed to cultivate respect for authority and for their peers. In this way, the school staff is more proactive in teaching its students about the ideals of respect, which have traditionally been part of their values and norms in the school. In addition to what appeared to be a missed opportunity to build up students' skills for those "unspoken" rules of school, the punishment prescribed for the pencil-throwing student seemed highly severe for the situation.

Overall, the student population is culturally diverse and economically disadvantaged, which contrasts with the teaching staff members, who are mostly White, non-Hispanic, middle-class females. This school's demographic as a whole is not uncommon in urban schools, as this typical staff and student makeup leads to most consultation relationships involving frames of reference that are similar between the consultant and consultee with clients who are culturally different (Kampwirth & Powers, 2012). Due to the marked cultural differences between the teaching staff and the students, cultural competence is a critical component for not only the consultation relationship but also for teachers who are working with culturally different students often in a cultural context that differs from their experiences.

Consultant–Consultee Relationship

The Initial Challenges of Collaborative Consultation

My first consultation relationship was established with Mrs. Experience, one of the two third-grade teachers at the school. She had been teaching for over 20 years at Sunshine Traditional Elementary School and was a White female teacher who was close to retirement. I was a mid-20s, White, first-year education specialist student. At the onset of the consultative relationship, I had hoped to establish a collaborative approach with Mrs. Experience, but I quickly realized that this frame of relationship would be difficult to establish. I established rapport with the teacher in our first meeting, and I empathized with her discussion about tough behaviors she was intervening with in her classroom, but Mrs. Experience seemed worn down by her students. Within our first consultation meeting, she spent a good majority of our time talking about one student who was exhibiting what she described as "extremely aggressive, out-of-control" classroom behavior. Some comments that she made implied that she viewed kids with a black-and-white mind-set and labeled them good or bad, like fruit selections in your local grocery store. For example, she would say things like "He's just a difficult boy" instead of saying something like "He exhibits challenging behavior." In this case, Mrs. Experience seemed to fail to recognize that there may be many ecological factors contributing to the behavior problems she was seeing played out in her classroom and instead attributed the child's behaviors to his overall character. Thus, Mrs. Experience displayed the type of consultee difficulty discussed by Ingraham (2000) as part of Component 2 in the multicultural school consultation (MSC) framework, in which there seems to be a lack of objectivity. It may be that her perspective was clouded by her inability to be positive about teaching and, more specifically, her class. At this point in the consultative relationship, I realized that Mrs. Experience engaged in judgment about her students at times without pausing to engage in mindful reflection of her students' behaviors. Dray and Wisneski (2011) have suggested that teachers take some time to mindfully reflect on their students' behaviors to explore alternative explanations for why they engage in them and to develop alternative plans for intervening with the behaviors. Instead of engaging in self-reflection of potential biases Mrs. Experience held about the student's behavior, Mrs. Experience expressed a sense of certainty that this was just a difficult student. As a novice consultant, I struggled to get her to be more open-minded about not only her student but also viewing the problem from a more ecological perspective. This resistance to evaluate personal impact on the individual student's behavior led to an increasing challenge to develop a positive plan to intervene with the behavior in the context of the consultative relationship.

In addition, at one point, Mrs. Experience was discussing this particular student and emphasized that she wanted to give him a "fresh start," but then a few minutes later disclosed to me that she just "didn't think he could make it." While the teacher did volunteer to participate, from the beginning of the consultation process there were signs of teacher resistance and lack of objectivity. Specifically regarding her outlook of the student she wanted to target with an intervention, Mrs. Experience exhibited signs of the "yes, but" resistance type as described by Kampwirth and Powers (2012) as agreeing that an idea has merit but asserting that it's not worth trying for some reason.

This type of resistance continued to become more and more evident throughout our relationship. As we approached the baseline phase, the teacher assured me that she had collected baseline data but never produced the data for me when I requested it several times. When I was attempting to organize the intervention implementation phase with her, I received a lot of communication avoidance from Mrs. Experience, such as her not returning my phone calls; making excuses for why I should not come to the school to meet on a day we had previously planned; and then her wanting to push back the implementation until after the kids returned from their spring break holiday, saying that they would be "too rowdy." At this point, in my role as a novice consultant I attempted to reduce resistance from Mrs. Experience as much as I could by trying to do all of the work required to implement the intervention myself in an attempt to reduce the consultee's effort. Unexpectedly, however, our consultation relationship came to an end rather abruptly due to Mrs. Experience e-mailing me to tell me that she would be absent from the school for just about the rest of the school year, with no explanation for her absence and with no suggestion of continuing the intervention planned for her classroom by collaborating with her substitute teacher for the remainder of the year.

A Second Chance at Collaborative Consultation

As a result of my first consultation relationship with Mrs. Experience ending rather abruptly, I then began a second consultation relationship with the other third-grade teacher at Sunshine Traditional Elementary School. Ms. Meredith was much different from Mrs. Experience in many ways. Primarily, the relationship was established out of Ms. Meredith's desire to engage in the implementation of a second intervention in her classroom, and she willingly volunteered to engage in the consultation process. My first meeting with Ms. Meredith, who was also White, was quite different from the meetings I had had with Mrs. Experience. Ms. Meredith was very warm, laid-back, and friendly. Her personality easily fit with the collaborative consultation approach I aspired to use in our relationship. In addition, about 50% of the students in Ms. Meredith's third-grade classroom had been identified as gifted and talented and subsequently required differentiated instruction, which provided Ms. Meredith with a great deal of experience in catering to the many individual needs represented in her classroom. I believe that having a familiarity with the practice of differentiated instruction and a firm foundational belief that there are many ecological factors and differences impacting each and every student in her classroom contributed to her viewing the students in a cultural context in that she understood their lived lives.

Communication Skills

Throughout my consultation relationship with Ms. Meredith, I used open-ended questioning. The use of this type of questioning really allowed me to get much more detail about the problem she was having in her classroom. It also helped to further build rapport with her since this type of questioning allows for more elaboration. I also found that this type of questioning fit nicely with Ms. Meredith's laid-back personality, as she was very eager to share the ideas and experiences she had had within her classroom. I found it very easy to match my communication style with that of Ms. Meredith, as we seemed to be quite similar in how we engaged in communication. With Ms. Meredith, it was also much more natural and easy for me to reflect a positive outlook on intervening with her classroom problem behaviors because she was so eager and receptive to working together to come up with an effective intervention for them. This was in stark contrast to the repeatedly negative perspective Mrs. Experience relayed about the students in her classroom, which made it difficult to approach intervention strategies with a positive outlook.

During our first meeting, there was one obstacle that came up. About halfway through our meeting, the school was issued a lockdown notice and we had to immediately cease our conversation to lock the windows, doors, and draw the shades; however, I used this downtime as an advantage to build more rapport with Ms. Meredith. We casually discussed her relationships with the students' parents, which gave me much insight into how she views her students collectively. But more importantly, her connection to parents demonstrates her understanding of the necessity of home–school collaboration.

Problem-Solving Process

Problem Identification

The problem-solving process used in the consultation with Ms. Meredith included the following steps: problem identification, problem analysis, plan implementation, and plan evaluation. When I first met with Ms. Meredith, she expressed concern over her students' ability to be productive during their math partner time, which they engage in about four days a week for approximately 30–40 min each day. When defining the problem, we actively explored what the root of this lack of productivity in their math partner work was. Ms. Meredith, during the problem analysis, felt that the major problem with the students' productivity was due to off-task behaviors they exhibited during partner time, such as talking about topics unrelated to the academic task, looking at materials unrelated to the task (chapter books for leisure reading), or just not communicating with their partner regarding the academic task. Therefore, the underlying issue for the students was their off-task behavior. Ms. Meredith and I spent a brief amount of time exploring intervention options because prior to beginning our consultative relationship, Ms. Meredith had become familiar with the Mystery Motivator intervention and was very interested in implementing this intervention in her classroom (Moore, Waguespack, Wickstrom, Witt, & Gaydos, 1994). In a way, it seemed as though the intervention had already been selected by Ms. Meredith prior to us identifying and clarifying the problem that was to be targeted with the intervention; however, the Mystery Motivator intervention actually was appropriate for the identified problem. It may be possible that the intervention Ms. Meredith was hoping to try actually fit with the problem identified due to Ms. Meredith's dedication to being in tune with the needs of her students and her willingness to research possible interventions on her own prior to beginning the consultative relationship. Her enthusiasm and familiarity with an intervention that fit appropriately with the problem identified also speaks to her willingness to explore new strategies to help her students in the classroom. This openness to change indicated to me that Ms. Meredith possessed flexibility in her practice, which was a further testament to her cultural competence as a teacher.

Once the problem was identified, Ms. Meredith and I worked together to collect baseline data. In order to collect baseline data, Ms. Meredith counted the number of math partner groups who met the daily math partner work standard. The daily math partner work standard was an explicit statement made by Ms. Meredith at the beginning of every math partner work session. Usually, the daily math partner work standard would be a simple completion goal such as "Complete math problem Numbers 1–5 on this math worksheet within 15 min in pairs." The students' attainment of the daily math partner work standard was based on their completion of the math problems rather than on accuracy. Baseline data were collected on 2 consecutive days. On the first day, only three groups achieved the daily work standard, and on the second day, four groups achieved the standard.

Next, Ms. Meredith and I worked together to develop a goal for the intervention based on the baseline data we had collected on the students' math partner time productivity. We decided that there would be an overall goal that we would like the students to meet at the closure of the intervention. The overall goal was that 75% of the math partner groups (pairs) would meet the daily math work standard. In order to reach that overall goal, we set smaller incremental goals for the students. The incremental goal was for the students to have five math partner groups meet the daily work standard to receive the reward, with the goal increasing incrementally as the students' productivity increased. This math partner goal was explicitly stated to the students each day at the beginning of their math partner work period in addition to the daily math work standard.

Intervention Design and Planning

The intervention design that Ms. Meredith and I agreed upon was a variation of the Mystery Motivator, which is a contingency-based reward system with a great degree of unpredictability (Moore et al., 1994). As emphasized by Rathvon (2008), the element of mystery and unpredictability, much like the mystery associated with a wrapped gift, is highly appealing to students and thus increases their motivation in completing the contingent behavior required to receive the reward. I created a poster with an envelope for each day of the week. I created about 20 different cards that could be placed in the envelopes, some with a classroom-wide reward written on them and some without a reward.

Ms. Meredith was concerned that the students might experience a meltdown if they did not receive a mystery reward but met the daily goal, so the compromise was that I wrote encouraging verbal praise statements on each and every card for the chart, regardless of whether or not a reward was presented on the card. I was pleased to see Ms. Meredith take ownership of the intervention strategy and tweak it so that it fit well with her classroom environment and her students' needs. This was an area where valuing the consultee's expertise of her individual students' needs and classroom strategies was highly critical. My act of supporting and incorporating this idea of Ms. Meredith's also helped to further strengthen the rapport between us. Ms. Meredith really wanted to have the intervention offer a classroom-wide reward because she highly values a sense of community in her classroom, so we incorporated a group contingency for earning the reward in which not all students had to meet the goal, just the specific number of math pairs that was the goal for the day. Ms. Meredith expressed that she felt that this method of reward would serve to have the students who were meeting the daily goal be peer models to the other students, modeling that they, too, could accomplish the goal to help the class, as a community, receive the reward. It was amidst these series of individualized tweaks made to the intervention that true collaboration was achieved between myself and the consultee. This collaboration process required a significant amount of trust up front and served to strengthen trust not just within the consultative relationship but also between the consultee and the client.

Intervention Implementation

The day following the end of baseline data collection, I visited Ms. Meredith's classroom to introduce the Mystery Motivator reward system to the students. I was, of course, well informed of the demonstrated success of the Mystery Motivator intervention due to its unpredictable nature, but—*wow!*—the students were incredibly intrigued about the potential rewards in the envelopes and probably would have asked me questions regarding the potential rewards for the rest of their school day had they been allowed. Ms. Meredith and I answered the students' questions as a team and emphasized that we could not tell them what rewards might be in the envelopes, but that they would have to first earn the privilege of opening an envelope to find out. Ms. Meredith then explicitly instructed the students that the goal for the day would be for five of the math partner groups to complete Problems 1–4 on a worksheet focusing on preparation for the state achievement tests that were coming up. The students met the goal the first day of the intervention, with six total groups meeting the daily math work standard. The following day, Ms. Meredith increased the math partner group goal to seven total groups in order to receive the reward. We did not discuss her increasing the group goal by 2 units, and I felt that increasing from five to seven might have been too large of a jump for the students, which could impact the effectiveness of the intervention. However, I also considered that Ms. Meredith knows her students' abilities much better than I do, and she may have believed that they could handle this increase. I may not have been clear about the importance of having a goal and how you evaluate the progress monitoring to see if the students reach the goal after several data points have been collected. On the third day the intervention was implemented, the goal for math partner groups was seven again, and only five of the groups met the goal. I decided at that point that my next step in meeting with Ms. Meredith would be to assess the students' progress. I considered that we might need to reduce the math partner goal in order to allow the students to experience success and receive the reward and then gradually increase the goal at a slow rate. Ms. Meredith had continued to implement the intervention for a few days before I was able to consult with her regarding lowering the goal number of groups. On the third day of having the goal set at seven groups, the class exceeded the goal with eight groups and received a reward. The next day, Ms. Meredith increased the goal once again to eight groups. After her class was unable to meet the goal during that day and the 2 following days, we were able to meet to discuss the progress of the intervention. Ms. Meredith was receptive to reducing the goal number of groups, especially since she was able to look at the data she had collected showing that the students were unable to reach the goal for 5 of the days she had implemented a higher goal. After we reduced the goal, the students were able to meet the goal again. Then, we gradually worked together to continually increase the goal, as more and more pairs of students were exceeding the goal for the daily math standard. My encouragement of Ms. Meredith to reconsider the goal she was setting for the students represented the delicate balance between practicing partnering and empathy versus the informing and guiding styles within the MSC framework (Ingraham, 2000). Up until this point in the consultative relationship, we had partnered together, and I did not feel like I had to take on the informant role at all; however, when the students were not succeeding with the intervention because I felt that the consultee may not have been able to consider the implications of her hurried increase in expectations on her own, I had to step into the role of carefully guiding a change in the intervention.

Evaluation

When I asked Ms. Meredith if she felt that the students were motivated by the intervention, she replied, "They love it!" This is critical, as Goldstein and Brooks (2007) assert that the level of student acceptability of the intervention plays a contributing role in effective behavior change. In turn, the level of student acceptability toward the intervention also influences the teacher's acceptability of the intervention. An important consideration with the intervention implementation is that I came into the classroom as an external "expert" from the students' perspective to introduce the intervention. This may have been a contributing factor to the overall success of the intervention. When Ms. Meredith and I met to discuss the overall result of the intervention based on the data we had collected, we reviewed our overall goal at the outset of implementing the intervention, which was for 75% of her students to meet the daily math work standard. At the closure of the Mystery Motivator intervention, a total of 11 pairs of students had met the daily math work standard, which was a total of 22 students out of the 28 students overall in her class. So, overall, the result was that 78% of Ms. Meredith's students had met the daily math work standard by the conclusion of the intervention, indicating a successful intervention.

Closure

As Ms. Meredith and I discussed the overall outcome of the Mystery Motivator intervention, we were both pleased with the success her students experienced in exhibiting more on-task behavior, which led to increased work completion of the daily math work standard. Ms. Meredith recognized in hindsight that a slower, more gradual increase in the goal for the students may have been a more positive approach and could have potentially led to greater success with the intervention since students may not have experienced as many days without receiving the reward through the Mystery Motivator. I found Ms. Meredith's realization that there was room for improvement in the goal-setting aspect of the intervention incredibly telling. First, she was able to evaluate her own actions' implications for the outcome of the intervention. In this way, I felt that Ms. Meredith's ability to self-reflect on intervention outcomes was closely tied with her overall cultural competence in her approach to teaching. I largely credited Ms. Meredith's insight regarding the group contingency and the use of positive reward statements on the envelopes that did not end up containing a tangible reward to leading to the over-all success of the Mystery Motivator intervention within her classroom with her community of students. In expressing this resolution to Ms. Meredith at the clo-sure of the consultative relationship, as well as my emphasis on her valued insights throughout the process, I worked to build consultee confidence and self-efficacy within the MSC framework (Ingraham, 2000).

I had requested that Ms. Meredith respond to a few questions about the consul-tation relationship and the intervention outcomes after our final meeting together via e-mail; however, I never received a response to these questions. I attributed this mainly to it being just 2 weeks before the end of the school year and assumed that there may have been many end-of-year tasks that Ms. Meredith had to attend to. Overall, Ms. Meredith and I maintained a positive consultative relationship that I felt was successful due to two elements: (a) Ms. Meredith's cultural competence in her relationship with students and (b) her willingness to engage in consultation from a collaborative approach.

Diversity Issues

Throughout my relationship with Ms. Meredith, diversity was not so much of an issue or barrier to consultation as it was an asset. Ms. Meredith's classroom is very diverse and different from her, with the majority of her students being Black, Multiracial, Asian American, or Hispanic. Ms. Meredith demonstrated exceptional clarity and effectiveness when it came to multicultural competence. She directly stated to me at one point that the students are much different than they used to be at the school, citing a population change that has resulted largely from a reduction in the amount of actual neighborhood children who enroll in Sunshine Traditional, as well as a movement of middle-class socio-economic status families out of the school district in general. A large majority of the children living in the neighborhood in which the school resides are now enrolled in private school programs both within and outside the neighborhood. Ms. Meredith also shared that because of the differences in today's students in her classroom compared with those who made up the student body at Sunshine just a few years before, she highly values the concept of explicitly teaching them behavioral expectations and how to carry themselves in the school environment. Jensen (2009) discusses using an inclusive approach to meet the need to experience belonging that is critical for children experiencing high poverty day to day. Ms. Meredith embodied this inclu-sivity with her community classroom approach and her drive to put the needs of the class as a whole before the needs of the individuals. As the consultant, it was quite refreshing to have the opportunity to work with such a culturally competent teacher who recognizes the need to directly address the usually unspoken rules of behavioral expectations of school that are lost so many times on children who come from high-poverty, urban backgrounds.

Another aspect of diversity that I observed in both of my novice consultant relationships was related to the culture and climate of each classroom I worked with. In Mrs. Experience's classroom, I discovered an individualistic culture that did not exude any real sense of community or connectedness. In contrast, I found in Ms. Meredith's classroom a collaborative, community approach to learning and development. Ms. Meredith shared at one point that while her students did not necessarily like each other at all times, they knew "how to deal with one another and keep their personal space when one student was having a bad day." Another element that spoke to this sense of community was an instance I observed where a parent entered the classroom in the middle of instruction to check the child out of school in order to take her to a medical exam. Instead of viewing this parent's entrance as a distraction or even just quietly addressing the parent, Ms. Meredith talked aloud to the class about the student leaving to go to her medical appointment and encouraged the classroom to wish her well as she left. Ms. Meredith exuded empathy and concern and displayed with her response that this student's well-being was infinitely more valued than any learning task that was going on in the classroom at the moment the parent entered to retrieve the student.

Lessons Learned

My opportunity to work with two different teachers who had very different approaches to teaching and personalities in general afforded me great insight into the process of collaborative consultation. First, with Mrs. Experience, I experienced firsthand the difficulties a consultant faces in effectively intervening when the teacher has a loss of objectivity about her students. Since I was in a novice consultant role, I was more reluctant to directly address and challenge some of her beliefs about her students. I do feel, however, that in my future role as a practicing school psychologist that in some cases it will not only be appropriate but necessary for me to develop and implement a tactful, supportive method for challenging negative, unfounded beliefs about students. A second insight I gained from working with Mrs. Experience was the importance of schedule flexibility. There were several occasions on which I wanted to conduct an observation of our initial target student, but the student was suspended. In addition, there were times when the consultee had forgotten about an appointment she had made on a day I was meeting with her or an impromptu meeting was convened with the school staff. This proved to be quite difficult, considering I was also balancing a work schedule and my class schedule as a graduate student; however, it helped me realize that even when I will be working in the schools full time, it will serve me well to be able to rearrange my schedule and be creative with how and when I meet with consultees.

In contrast, while working with Ms. Meredith, I learned quite different lessons. With Ms. Meredith, I learned to be inspired by the different perspective that can be offered by teachers when it comes to interventions. Ms. Meredith's idea to include written praise statements on the Mystery Motivator reward cards was a positive addition to the Mystery Motivator intervention. This also helped me actualize valuing the perspective of the teacher and incorporating her individual ideas when it comes to creating and implementing the intervention. I think this helps to build mutual respect and trust within the consultant–consultee relationship. I also learned that the consultee's teaching style may play a critical role in the overall effectiveness of an intervention. Ms. Meredith possesses a very interactive, supportive teaching style that lends itself nicely to the interactive factor of the Mystery Motivator intervention. She also seemed to buy in to the intervention, which helped her provide motivation and excitement for the students with the intervention. Perhaps most importantly, Ms. Meredith's strong ability to perceive and understand her students within a cultural context, I think, helped her to see that her students would be more motivated as a community of learners in the intervention, which was achieved through our establishing a group contingency for the Mystery Motivator reward. And, finally, I learned the importance of conveying how each aspect of the problem-solving model needs to be meticulously followed. Ms. Meredith's choice to change the goal early without consulting with me put a small wrinkle in the intervention. Fortunately, we were able to correct it.

In conclusion, the contrast of my experiences in working with Mrs. Experience and Ms. Meredith over the semester provided me with much insight into how various consultee factors play into the success and effectiveness of the consultant–consultee relationship. It also reinforced the importance for me as a consultant to be well versed in strategies that can be used to intervene with various forms of resistance and consultee beliefs that can and will arise throughout the course of a consultant–consultee relationship.

Questions for Reflection

- How could the novice consultant have challenged some of the negative beliefs Mrs. Experience held about her students' behaviors? What communication strategies would you have used to introduce discussion about ecological factors influencing her students' behaviors?
- Is there anything you would have done differently as a consultant when met with resistance from Mrs. Experience? In what other ways might a more experienced consultant have responded to the abrupt end of the consultation relationship with Mrs. Experience?

- When considering the consultation relationship between the consultant and Ms. Meredith, what characteristics did Ms. Meredith possess that led to the success of the intervention? In contrast, were there any identifiable barriers Ms. Meredith brought to the consultation relationship?

References

Dray, B. J., & Wisneski, D. B. (2011). Mindful reflection as a process for developing culturally responsive practices. *Teaching Exceptional Children, 44*, 28–36.

Goldstein, S., & Brooks, R. B. (2007). *Understanding and managing children's classroom behavior: Creating sustainable, resilient classrooms.* Hoboken, NJ: Wiley & Sons.

Greene, R. W. (2008). *Lost at school: Why our kids with behavioral challenges are falling through the cracks and how we can help them.* New York, NY: Scribner.

Ingraham, C. L. (2000). Consultation through a multicultural lens: Multicultural and cross-cultural consultation in schools. *School Psychology Review, 29*, 320–343.

Jensen, E. (2009). *Teaching with poverty in mind: What being poor does to kids' brains and what schools can do about it.* Alexandria, VA: Association for Supervision and Curriculum Development.

Kampwirth, T. J., & Powers, K. M. (2012). *Collaborative consultation in the schools: Effective practices for students with learning and behavior problems.* Upper Saddle River, NJ: Pearson Education.

Moore, L. A., Waguespack, A. M., Wickstrom, K. F., Witt, J. C., & Gaydos, G. R. (1994). Mystery Motivator: An effective and time efficient intervention. *School Psychology Review, 23*, 106–118.

Rathvon, N. (2008). *Effective school interventions.* New York, NY: Guilford Press.

12

SUMMARY AND CONCLUSION

Antoinette Halsell Miranda

My goal for this book was to provide readers with a variety of cases that demonstrate how using a multicultural school consultation (MSC) framework can address issues of diversity that potentially can be a barrier to the consultation process, as well as how it can contribute to a successful outcome. Case studies were chosen to demonstrate the application of the MSC framework, as they have been identified as an effective tool for improving the learning experience by applying knowledge to a relevant situation. They are a form of problem-based learning that allows the learner to practice and apply new concepts. Many of these cases are context driven and can actually have multiple solutions. Too often, issues of diversity are ignored in the work we do with students in schools. However, I think that this is most often driven by a lack of knowledge in how to approach issues of diversity as well as the fear of opening a can of worms. The reality is that until we dig deeper into the cultural context in which students exist, we will struggle to find solutions that will truly make a difference in the lives of marginalized children.

Nine case studies examined issues of diversity at both the macro- and the microlevel. The novice consultants provided insight into their own thinking and choices made during the consultation process as they navigated unfamiliar territory in urban classrooms and with diverse students. While some were challenged with contextual issues such as poverty or cultural dynamics in the classroom, others had to contemplate the relationship between themselves and a consultee who was disconnected from his or her students. For example, McClure reflected on how identifying with her consultee "too much" may have contributed to him believing that she agreed with the many negative comments he made regarding the students in his class. As a novice consultant, she was challenged with her role on how to intervene to change the narrative. Wargelin and Mallen found their consultee to be a cultural mediator who provided background and explanations for behavior, based on the consultee's experience, with respect to working with the African American girls in her classroom. While they were committed to the intervention chosen, they quickly realized that they lacked a cultural connection and knowledge of some of the issues unique to young African American girls. Thus, to increase their knowledge base, they reached out to their consultee, who was African American, as well as other African American women who helped them with the implementation of the intervention. As a result, they increased their cultural competency as well as their personal connections and relationships with the young girls in their intervention group. In Part IV, the novice consultants were fortunate to engage in the consultation process with teachers who demonstrated cultural competency. With these consultees, they often found it easy to talk about issues of race and social class but, more importantly, the discussions helped them have a deeper understanding of the issues or problems being addressed in the consultation process. It is interesting to note that only these cases had successful outcomes for their interventions. Not only did the consultants find the consultees to be culturally competent, but the consultees also had many characteristics of effective teachers that most likely contributed to the successful implementations of the interventions as well.

Several of the contributing novice consultants reflected on their experience:

> Writing this chapter on the MSC framework has truly changed my outlook on consultation in the schools. It is so much more complex and confusing than I had previously thought as a novice consultant. It really opened my eyes to the necessity of understanding yourself before you can understand, and even help, others. Even more so, how important it is to effect change on a systems level rather than an individual level—this is absolutely critical if we want to change the way society views and shapes those in the education system, thus improving the overall well-being of so many marginalized children in our nation's schools.

> The consultation experience itself, as well as the reflective process I engaged in while writing my book chapter, was incredibly instructive. In particular, this consultation case made me reflect upon teachers whose students hail from different cultural backgrounds and how consultants can apply the MSC framework to aid these teachers in increasing their self-awareness and encouraging them to create more meaningful relationships with their students. By leveraging their own self-awareness and better understanding of their students, teachers can work to implement effective multicultural practices within their classrooms.

> Writing the chapter was an excellent experience because it challenged me to delve deeper into the MSC framework for school consultation. The more I explored my consultation case, the more I realized that I still had much to learn. Student diversity affects classrooms in complex ways, and

> I know that this experience has prepared me to think critically about class-room diversity in the future.
>
> Writing this chapter furthered both my knowledge and integration of the MSC framework in both my personal life and career. I think at a greater depth about how different instances of diversity influence my thoughts, expectations, and behaviors and look for ways to provide reference points to bridge differences or establish connections across various cultures or issues of diversity, especially in consultation practices.

Their reflections capture both the complexity of the consultation process using the ecological model and the MSC framework, as well as thoughts about how the consultants could do things differently in the future. The cases provided them the opportunity to practice skills taught in class, often with the accompanying realization that it was much harder than they thought. They discovered that the awareness and knowledge gained in the diversity class the semester before became an invaluable tool as they contemplated their own cultural awareness in relation to their cases, as well as the cultural complexities evident in the schools and the communities in which the students resided.

It is hoped that readers will use the case studies as a teaching tool for the application of the MSC framework to real-world situations. Reflection questions at the beginning and end of each chapter that are focused on the consultation process as well as issues of diversity are designed to stimulate dialogue, explore alternative solutions, and build the consultant's problem-solving skills as they relate broadly to diversity issues. It is recognized that just because a student has a diverse background does not necessarily mean that there will be challenges with the consultation process—quite the contrary, as most cases in the consultation class did not have a glaring diversity issue. It is fair to say that many of the cases, however, did have issues of diversity that indirectly impacted the case. For example, many of the urban schools had discipline policies in which students were frequently suspended. As a result, there were cases in which the intervention was delayed or interrupted because the student was absent due to a suspension. Thus, this issue is a systems issue that a consultant could address, especially if the data suggest an overreliance on out-of-school punishment that leads to a disproportionality for African American and Latino males as it relates to suspension.

The inequities and challenges in education are real and ones that researchers, educators, and legislators are trying to "fix." At a time when our school-age population is increasingly diverse, it is critical that we explore effective ways to provide quality and equitable educational services to the most marginalized students in our schools. As we continue to find solutions to what sometimes seems like an intractable problem, it is imperative that we at least train our education professionals to be aware and knowledgeable about issues of diversity, societal influences, and the sociocultural context of students in American schools. This awareness and knowledge are foundational for developing change agents who are driven to provide services that effectively change the trajectory of so many students' educational lives. I believe that the work we do in schools, especially with the most vulnerable students, should embrace a social justice perspective. The work of the social justice change agent is consistent with utilizing the MSC framework, as it encourages an ecological perspective in identifying how best to address students' needs. Embracing CARE—cultural competency, advocacy, relationship building, and empowering and engaging—is at the core of socially just practice using an MSC framework. School-based consultants are often in a position to influence teachers and administrators on best practice when intervening with students from a variety of backgrounds. Their ability to use the MSC framework to build bridges, identify cultural uniqueness, and contribute greater articulation of cultural issues will be beneficial in finding solutions that are culturally relevant and responsive (Ingraham, 2000).

It is hoped that this book of case studies will assist school-based consultants in learning how to operationalize the MSC framework and understand how it can guide them through the successful implementation of interventions, addressing issues of diversity up front so that they are not a barrier to meeting the needs of students. Engaging in culturally responsive practices is a best practice.

Reference

Ingraham, C. L. (2000). Consultation through a multicultural lens: Multicultural and cross-cultural consultation in schools. *School Psychology Review, 29*, 320–343.

CONTRIBUTORS

Abigail Baillie is a school psychology intern in Southwestern City Schools and is completing her EdS degree in school psychology at The Ohio State University. During her internship year, she is looking forward to working more with teachers and developing her consultation skills within the schools. After graduation, she hopes to work as a full-time school psychologist, specifically with students from urban populations.

Maggie Beard is a fourth-year PhD school psychology student at The Ohio State University. She is looking forward to implementing multicultural approaches in schools and clinics. After graduation, she hopes to integrate research with practice to inform school psychology practice, policy, and procedures.

Amy Bremer is a doctoral school psychology student at The Ohio State University. She is currently a school psychologist in Columbus City Schools, a large urban district. After graduation, Amy will be working full time as a school psychologist for Columbus City Schools.

Nicole M. Brown is a fourth-year PhD student at The Ohio State University. She is looking forward to continuing her research related to mental health and social justice and specifically working on her dissertation involving youth with autism and bullying in the schools. After graduation, she hopes to work as a full-time school psychologist working with students and families from urban populations.

Kristen N. Heering is currently a school psychologist in Mississippi. Kristen is looking forward to extending a collaborative multicultural approach to consultation with rural populations in Mississippi, where she hopes to bring more awareness to mental health issues and social justice in the schools.

Colette L. Ingraham is a professor in the school psychology program at San Diego State University. She specializes in multicultural and cross-cultural school consultation, systemic school interventions, and multicultural issues. Her research interests include (a) consultation in culturally diverse schools, (b) systems change and comprehensive service delivery, and (c) developing professional leaders.

Jennifer Kong is a bilingual school psychologist in the New York City Department of Education. She provides support to children and families from culturally diverse backgrounds. Her scholarly interests are in multicultural consultation.

Emilia C. Lopez is a professor and director of the bilingual and multicultural specializations in the school psychology program at Queens College, City University of New York. Her scholarly work is focused on bilingual and multicultural school psychology practices.

McKenzie Mallen is a school psychology intern in the Gahanna City School District and is completing her EdS degree in school psychology at The Ohio State University. Her professional interests include working with urban students to develop social–emotional skills. McKenzie is looking forward to graduation and working as a full-time school psychologist.

Erin M. McClure is a fourth-year PhD student at The Ohio State University (OSU). After receiving dual bachelor's degrees in the areas of psychology and criminology and her master's degree in education at OSU, she is now pursuing her doctoral degree in school psychology. Erin is employed as a behavior consultant working alongside a licensed psychologist in the Columbus, Ohio, area.

Antoinette Halsell Miranda is a professor in the school psychology program at The Ohio State University. Her research interests include developing effective interventions with at-risk children in urban settings, consultation services in urban settings, and the development of racial identity and its relationship to academic achievement. Dr. Miranda has been committed to issues of social justice, especially equality of opportunity for marginalized students in school settings.

Kisha M. Radliff is an associate professor in the school psychology program at The Ohio State University teaching the mental health sequence, the school neuropsychology course, and the school- and clinical-based practica. She is committed to social justice issues, particularly in the context of mental health and school psychology training.

Naima Shirdon is a fourth-year doctoral student in school psychology at The Ohio State University. She believes in the value of consultation services in promoting data-based decision making and multicultural practice. She is currently consulting with a teacher in an urban school on student- and classroom-level issues. She hopes to continue her consultancy work after earning her doctorate to advance social justice efforts.

Carly Tindall is currently working toward her PhD in school psychology at Loyola University Chicago. She is looking forward to gaining more experience in working with at-risk student populations and researching issues experienced in urban education. Upon graduation, she aspires to gain licensure as a psychologist and contribute to the field of school psychology through research and teaching at the university level.

Lauren Wargelin is a third-year doctoral student at The Ohio State University. Her research interests include academic interventions and applications of positive psychology to school settings. After graduation, she hopes to obtain a faculty position so she can help future school psychologists develop their professional skills.

INDEX